Ernest H. Sims

Boatbuilding in Aluminium Alloy

First published by
NAUTICAL PUBLISHING COMPANY LIMITED
Nautical House, Lymington, Hampshire, England

in association with
George G. Harrap and Company Limited, London

March 1978

ISBN 0 245 5 31289

Filmset and printed in Great Britain by
BAS Printers Limited, Over Wallop, Hampshire

Foreword

By T. E. B. Sopwith

My introduction to aluminium race boats came in 1969, when I drove the first boat that the author was responsible for at John Goulandris' Enfield Marine yard. For a first attempt the boat was highly successful, not only winning a World Championship event at its second attempt, but also gaining the prize for the first circuit of the Isle of Wight in under an hour.

Both Don Shead, who designed the boat, and I were most impressed with the idea of aluminium construction, and the following year Miss Enfield II was runner-up in the World Championship, although we competed in many fewer races than that year's champion.

I lay no claim to being a marine engineer or boat builder, but I have been most impressed with the aluminium boats that I have driven.

The quality of the Enfield race boats was perhaps a reflection of the great enthusiasm that Ernie Sims showed for building in aluminium, and their durability was certainly the tribute to his competence in this field and indeed to the expertise of the workforce that he trained at Wootton Creek. If I were to be involved with another race boat in the future it would in all probability be of aluminium construction. I am delighted to have been given the chance to write this piece, as I look back with great pleasure on the years that Ernie Sims and I worked together during the Enfield competition programme, and I wish him, and indeed this book, every possible success.

Contents

Acknowledgements

My thanks must be put on record to John Goulandris for providing me with the opportunity to experiment and to develop construction techniques which up to that time were totally unknown to us; to the members of the team of Enfield Marine Ltd. who by their ingenuity and perseverance overcame some seemingly impossible problems, the fruits of some of which are here-in recorded.

To Tommy Sopwith who contributed a wealth of experience during his period as driver of the Enfield Offshire Race Boats. His criticisms were always constructive and helpful.

To Don Shead and his team who provided most of the design know-how; he was always ready with a sympathetic ear and a quick response to any construction problems.

I am grateful to the British Aluminium Company Technical Department for reading the original manuscript, and making some valuable suggestions in the chapter on corrosion.

My special thanks to Jeffrey Please who provided the cutaway drawing, and many of the photographs; to my daughter Wendy who made such an excellent job of the typing, and to the following companies for providing information and illustrations;

Tucker Fasteners Ltd. Birmingham.

Insley Industrial Ltd. Bracknell.

Westinghouse Electrical Corporation U.S.A.

International Paints.

Alcan Ltd. Banbury.

My thanks also to Erroll Bruce for his encouragement and patience. It takes a lot of faith to publish a first off, I hope his faith is justified.

List of Illustrations

Introduction

So much misconception and apparent mystery surrounds the construction, use and history of the marine applications of aluminium alloys and so little advice or instruction exists that this alone would justify adding yet another volume to the already bulging bookshelves of those whose livelihood depends upon satisfying the demands of the private and public sector for marine craft and the ever increasing marine applications.

There can by now be little doubt that most people engaged in the boatbuilding industry recognise that there is a use for aluminium alloys. The dilemma is; where, when, what and how. This book endeavours to answer some of the questions. It is not an exhaustive study; it is presumed the reader has a knowledge of boatbuilding and may well be currently engaged professionally in supplying boats in the 30-ft. to 130-ft. range, and finds that his customers have demands that cannot be met by the use of his existing practices. There are, unquestionably, types of craft and other applications where aluminium alloys will perform their function in a way that is superior to all other materials. Just as wood, plastic and steel are in turn superior in their own specialist application.

Because of the higher basic material costs, an aluminium boat may cost initially somewhat more than a similar steel vessel. There are, however, savings over a period of years that would justify the increased cost and could result in a nett gain. It has been variously calculated that a weight saving of between 35 and 45% can be expected from the use of aluminium alloys as against steel for hulls, and between 55 and 65% for superstructures. The advantage gained by the weight saving can be capitalised by an increase in speed for the same engine h.p. or a reduction in engine h.p. for the same speed. Maintenance costs are considerably reduced; there is no oxide bleeding—i.e., rusting, when the paint film deteriorates or is damaged. An aluminium hull requires no painting except for anti-fouling and for decorative reasons. It will never be necessary to indulge in the time consuming and plate thickness reducing task of rust chipping. If constructed of the proper alloys, an aluminium boat can be neglected to a far greater extent than the majority of all other materials, provided that where dissimilar metals are in close association with the hull, sacrificial anodes are maintained.

In the writer's experience, it has been more beneficial to introduce wood boatbuilders to the use of aluminium alloys than to use operators with an existing experience in steel fabrication. The former has a delicacy of touch that does not always exist in the latter.

Many of the wood boatbuilder's tools can also be used on aluminium. Few of the steel man's tools are suitable.

Methods and techniques of shaping and forming differ fundamentally from those used with steel.

Whereas with steel, the effort is put into heating, hammering and forcing, with aluminium, cold shrinking and stretching provides better results. The material being more ductile, responds to more gentle treatment.

Larger bend radii are necessary; consequently, different knives are used on bending machines.

Welding machines and techniques can be quite different from the normal welding for steel.

There are, of course, also certain disadvantages in the use of aluminium alloys and these should not be overlooked, although the rate of imbalance is improving rapidly. There are still a great many more welding repair facilities for steel than for aluminium. On the larger vessels, with adequate electricity generating equipment, a small M.I.G. or T.I.G. set could be carried which would be sufficient for all but the major problems, or a shore electricity supply could be connected. A drill and a supply of rivets should be part of the boat's stores. This would enable temporary repairs at least to be effected. (See chapter 18 on repairs). A selection of various thicknesses of aluminium offcuts should be readily obtainable from the building yard. It would indeed be prudent to have the building yard make up a repair kit consisting of all necessary items relevant to a repair of any kind.

Aluminium has a fairly low melting point about 1100°F. Consequently in high risk areas, fire protection must be considered (see chapter 16).

There are certain items of marine chandlery that are not compatible with aluminium. This is rapidly righting itself as more and more fittings of a basic aluminium nature are becoming available, and provided the proper precautions, as discussed in later chapters, are taken, even dissimilar metals can be used in proximity to one another without a disastrous effect.

Aluminium is a very clean material and there are no dirty processes. It is comparatively light weight, therefore easily handled. Operators like working with the material; working processes, welding, cutting, drilling, shaping, forming etc., are generally quicker than with steel; therefore, production costs are lower. The cost of production equipment is higher, but the effect of wear and tear is somewhat less. Saw blades are cheaper and last longer, all cutting and drilling equipment maintains a sharper edge for a longer period. Cold shaping with the correct shrinking and stretching tools (see chapter 3 on tools) is remarkably quick and effective. Storage of aluminium creates less problems than steel; there is less weight and less deterioration to consider.

There are many thousands of sections for which extrusion dies are available. These include angles, channels, tees, zeds, 'I' beams, solid squares, flat bars, hollow rectangles, solid rounds, polygons, hollow hexagons, quarter rounds, beading, fillets, half round mouldings, step edges, corner mouldings, fluted strip and fluted angles, cover mouldings, water channels, drip mouldings, as well as a great variety of tube diameters and wall thicknesses.

If a special extrusion is required, it is no great expense to have a die especially produced, depending on the quantity to be extruded.

A designer needs to prepare himself for the design of aluminium structures; design parameters and functions that have proved satisfactory in steel are not readily convertible into aluminium. The design criteria is different, and should be recognised as such, just as the builder in turn must learn that aluminium is like no other material, and to obtain the maximum from it, he must adjust to its own peculiarities and characteristics. The owner too has a part to play if he wishes to get a maximum return from his investment. He must appreciate that aluminium dents and gouges more easily than steel. He must recognise the natural laws that exist in relation to the metal and are herein explained.

1 Aluminium and its Alloys

The discovery of the element aluminium was made in the early part of the 19th century. At first, it was very difficult and extremely costly to extract, and isolate very tiny particles from the basic bauxite. In the mid 19th century the method of isolation changed, using sodium instead of potassium, enabling larger particles to be formed. This in turn was improved upon when metallic aluminium was produced by dissolving alumina in a molten cryolite, obtaining about twenty-two percent alumina, then passing electric currents through the solution. As a result, the production costs fell to a fraction of what they had been.

The method of extraction widely used today is known as the Electrolytic Reduction Process. Fundamentally, this is brought about by the breaking down of alumina into aluminium and oxygen. Oxygen combining with carbon at the anode, is released as carbon dioxide gas. As cryolite melts at around 980°C and the aluminium at around 650°C, the process is continuous. It has been estimated that it requires about 20,000 kilowatt hours of electricity to produce a ton of aluminium, and about four tons of bauxite to make two tons of alumina, the whole process producing about one ton of metallic aluminium. During the process about 1,500 pounds of carbon electrodes are also consumed. It is evident from this that the production of aluminium is a highly complex and expensive operation. The most commercially pure aluminium has a very limited use, being rather soft and weak, with a tensile strength of between 4 and 6 tons per square inch. Its use is normally limited to spinning, and deep draws of a complex shape.

To produce a material having the corrosion resistance of aluminium, and at the same time being commercially acceptable by having higher strength values, it is necessary to alloy with the aluminium, various other metals, each introduced for a very specific purpose. This is what we know as aluminium alloy.

There are many designated alloys of aluminium. Each one is produced to fulfil a specific need for a specific industry. We shall concern ourselves only with those alloys that have a special interest in a marine application.

The following are some of the metals used in varying proportions in the alloying process: copper, magnesium, silicon, iron, manganese, zinc, and chromium. The percentages used are small and vary with the physical requirements of the finished product. For our purposes, the greatest single element is magnesium with between four and five percent. For most of the others, it can vary between 0.1 and 1.0 percent. The remainder, of course, is aluminium.

In general, there are two types of wrought alloy: (a) non-heat-treatable, and (b) heat-treatable.

(a) *Non-heat-treatable alloys*
The non-heat-treatable wrought alloys are indicated by the initial letter 'N'. These alloys can be strengthened only by cold working and are softened by heating. The tempers or conditions in which they may be obtained range from soft or annealed temper to the fully work hardened condition.

Temper is indicated by the following symbols:

O	Material in the annealed condition.
M	Material in the 'as manufactured' conditions—e.g., as rolled, as extruded or drawn to size.
H1, H2 H3, H4 H5, H6 H7, H8	Strain hardened material subjected to the application of cold work after annealing or to a combination of cold work and partial annealing in order to secure the specified mechanical properties. The designations are in ascending order of tensile strength.

It is normal to use the non-heat-treatable alloys in the O or M condition where much forming or welding is to be applied. As these alloys do not depend on heat treatment to achieve their mechanical properties, they can be reheated without any appreciable loss of strength. Also, they can be cold worked much more efficiently than the heat-treatable alloys.

(b) *Heat-treatable alloys*
The heat-treatable wrought alloys are indicated by the initial letter H, and condition is described by the following suffix symbols:

O M	As for non-heat-treatable alloys
T	Material which has been solution treated and requires no precipitation treatment
T.D.	Solution heat-treated, cold worked and naturally aged.
T.E.	Cooled from an elevated temperature shaping process and precipitation-treated.
WP or TF	Solution heat-treated and precipitation treated.
T.H.	Solution heat-treated cold worked and then precipitation treated.
P	Material which has been precipitation treated only.

Thus a single heat-treatment alloy in its strongest condition is indicated by the suffix T, and a double-heat-treatment alloy by the suffix W.P.

Heat treatment

There are three types of heat treatment that are commonly applied to aluminium alloys: (1) Annealing, (2) Solution treatment, (3) Ageing treatment.

(1) *Annealing*
A period of half to four hours at temperatures between 350 and 380°C is sufficient to soften aluminium alloys for cold working or to relieve internal stress. The longer times and higher temperatures are advisable for the medium and high strength alloys when maximum softness is required. The rate of cooling from the annealing temperature has a considerable influence on the final hardness. Cooling in still air is satisfactory for most purposes, but for the lowest possible hardness the material should be cooled in the furnace at a controlled rate of less than 20°C per hour until the temperature is below 200°C.

(2) *Solution treatment*
Solution treatment consists of heating for periods of from half to twenty-four hours at prescribed temperatures between 460 and 545°C. The material is then quenched. The mechanical properties of most alloys are improved to varying degrees by solution treatment. The tensile strength and proof stress are considerably increased over the properties in the annealed condition but the elongation is usually reduced. In comparison to the 'as wrought' condition, the improvement after solution treatment applies to all three properties. The temperature of the water of the quench has a considerable effect on the mechanical properties of the degree of internal stress. The cold water quench gives maximum mechanical properties, but the advantage is offset by the introduction of high internal stress. The boiling water quench leaves less residual strength and reduces the risk of distortion but the strength and hardness are lower.

(3) *Ageing treatment*
The improvement in strength following solution treatment can be further increased by ageing or precipitation. Some alloys begin to harden rapidly at room temperature immediately after quenching. Although the process slows down after a few hours, the maximum improvement in strength and hardness is approached after five days. For many alloys ageing at room temperature does not produce the best properties and a treatment at temperatures between 120 and 215°C is necessary.

The heat-treatable alloys then are the most difficult to form. But, almost because of that, they may be considered most suitable for longitudinals, stringers, etc., inasmuch as, because of their resistance to shaping, they may produce a fairer line, provided the shape is not complex or excessive. Even here, however, it is possible to provide local heat to aid severe forming. A good method is to use acetylene oxygen with a large, soft flame rather than the hard oxygen flame. Care must be exercised not to concentrate the heat in one spot, but spread over a fairly large area. It is possible, also, that the strength properties would be affected.

The material considered by many authorities to be the most suitable for boat construction exterior use, is for plate to British Standard Specification 1477 NP8 and for extrusions B.S. 1476 NE8. This is a magnesium alloy with the following characteristics:

Strength:	Medium (tensile about 18 tons per sq. in.)
Ductility:	High
Formability:	Very good
Corrosion resistance:	Excellent
Weldability:	Very good

For superstructures a stronger sheet material could be used with advantage, such as B.S. 1470 NS6 H2 or H3, depending on the amount of forming. This has a higher proof stress, and would produce a stiffer panel in the thinner sheet gauges.

It should be, and often is, the responsibility of the designer to stipulate the type and grade of aluminium alloy to be used. Occasionally, the builder has to decide, either because the designer has not so specified, or because the materials originally specified are not available, and a substitute must be accepted. In these circumstances, the builder should provide himself with a good working knowledge of the characteristics of the various alloys and their conditions. The aluminium manufacturers are always very generous in their advice and literature, and advantage should be taken of this.

2 Design for Construction

This book does not attempt to cover the subject of design, which is discussed in various other publications, although it is possible that naval architects not already familiar with constructing in aluminium alloy may benefit from a knowledge of the practices on the shop floor.

An attempt has been made to provide the designer with some background knowledge of how to exploit the use of the material to its full potential and at the same time to realise its limitations so that the boatbuilder is not asked to spend unnecessary hours trying to attain the impossible.

To obtain the maximum advantage of using aluminium either in part or as a whole, the designer must be aware of the physical characteristics of the material. In this way, he can design a structure for maximum efficiency. For all practical purposes, aluminium, like other metals, is of a homogeneous nature, and the physical characteristics of each different aluminium alloy are known and readily available from the manufacturer. It must be emphasised, though, that this applies in the as supplied condition. In the non-heat-treatable alloys such as are normally used for hull plates, heating has little effect upon these characteristics. But in the heat-treatable alloys, which to some extent gain their strength from a heat process, the characteristics can be affected adversely by the further application of heat.

Comparative properties with other materials is illustrated in figure A-1. These are general figures and should only be used as such.

Because it is possible to design to precise safety factors and thereby produce a very light hull, it is all the more important that these safety factors are not eroded by action on the shop floor. This indicates that a degree of quality control should emanate from the designer. It also indicates that the designer must provide a greater amount of detailed information to the shop floor. For this purpose, and to familiarise himself with the problems met at operator level, the designer should spend, particularly in his formative years, as much time on the shop floor as can be spared. The custom of 'coming up through the shop floor' has declined over recent years, to the detriment of the future designer. It is in the interest of all concerned that, if the material is to be exploited to the full, the designer must appreciate the total concept and be in a position to advise on shop floor problems, whilst at the same time, not demanding extreme or unnecessary standards.

Aluminium alloys have a high resistance to shock, provided that a notch or sharp change of section with its attendant stress concentration is avoided. Sharp

COMPARATIVE PROPERTIES OF MATERIALS

MATERIAL	WEIGHT PER CU. FT. (LB)	COEFFICIENT OF EXPANSION X 10-6/° F.	MODULUS OF ELASTICITY X 10^6 LB/SQ. INCH	APPROXIMATE STRENGTH IN TENSION TONS / SQ. INCH		GALVANIC OR CHEMICAL EFFECT ON UNPROTECTED ALUMINIUM
				ULTIMATE	PROOF OR YIELD	
ALUMINIUM ALLOY D54S M	165	13	10	17 (MIN)	8 (MIN)	NONE
STRUCTURAL STEEL (B.S. 15)	489	6½	29	28 - 33	16 (MIN)	MILD
HIGH TENSILE STEEL (B.S. 968)	489	6½	29	32 - 39	23 (MIN)	MILD
STAINLESS STEEL (18-8)	498	9½	29	35 - 45	14 - 17	NONE
BRASS (60-40) (B.S. 1949)	580	10½	15	20 (MIN)	10 (MIN)	SEVERE
COPPER	556	9½	17	14 - 16	-	SEVERE
PHOSPHOR BRONZE (5% SN)	552	10	16	22 - 48	10 - 45	SEVERE
ALUMINIUM BRONZE (5% AL)	510	9½	17 - 19	25	-	SEVERE
K MONEL (67 NI : 30 CU)	554	8	26	31 - 62	11 - 58	SEVERE
LEAD (ROLLED)	710	16	2½	1	½	MILD
ZINC (ROLLED)	445	22	6	10	2	PROTECTIVE
HARD WOODS	35 - 60	-	1 - 3½	2 - 15 (COMP)	-	MILD
SOFT WOODS	25 - 35	-	1 - 2	2 - 7 (COMP)	-	MILD

A-1 *Comparative properties of materials.*

radii, undercuts, abrupt change of section and other stress raisers should be avoided in highly stressed areas. It is probable that unsuspected stress concentrations, and locked up stresses, are responsible for many failures, and material selection can do little to alleviate such troubles. Such stress concentrations cannot always be avoided, but every endeavour should be made by designers to reduce their effect as far as possible.

The prevention of fatigue is a matter of correct selection of material and careful design. There is a far greater latitude for improvement in the design field than is generally appreciated.

Aluminium alloy manufacturers provide figures for the mechanical properties of the various grades and tempers of their product. It may be worthwhile defining what these terms relate to.

The tensile properties usually quoted are the tensile strength, the 0·1% proof stress and the elongation.

These terms are defined in B.S. 18:1962 as follows:

(1) *Tensile strength*
The tensile strength is the maximum load under the prescribed testing conditions divided by the original cross sectional area of the gauge length of the test piece.

(2) *Proof stress*
Proof stress is the stress (load divided by the original area of the cross-section of a test piece) which is just sufficient to produce, under load, a non-proportional elongation equal to a specified percentage of the extensometer gauge length.

(3) *Percentage elongation*

This is given by $\frac{(Lu-Lo)\,100}{Lo}$

Where Lo = original gauge length

Lu = distance between the original gauge marks obtained by measurement of the fractured test piece.

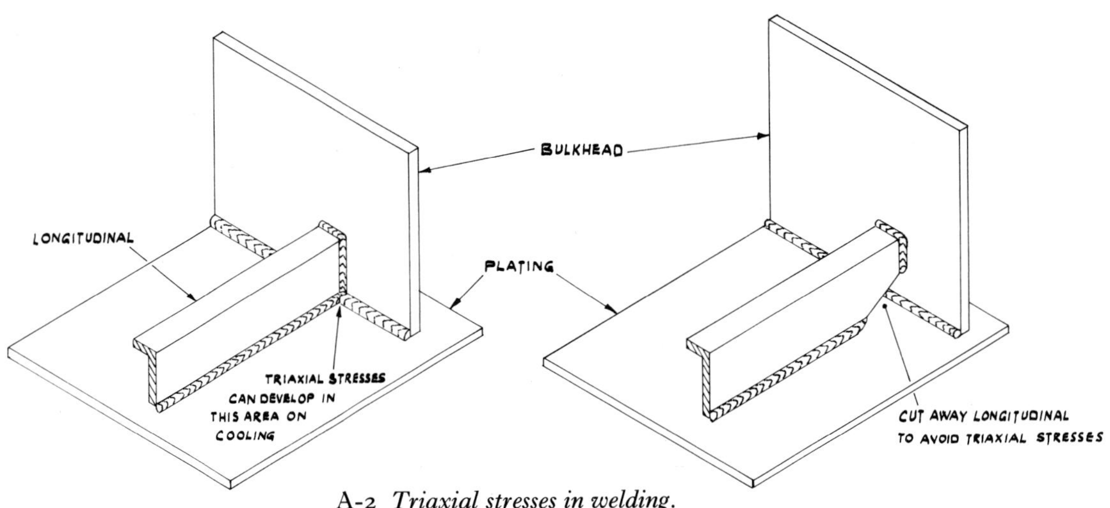

A-2 *Triaxial stresses in welding.*

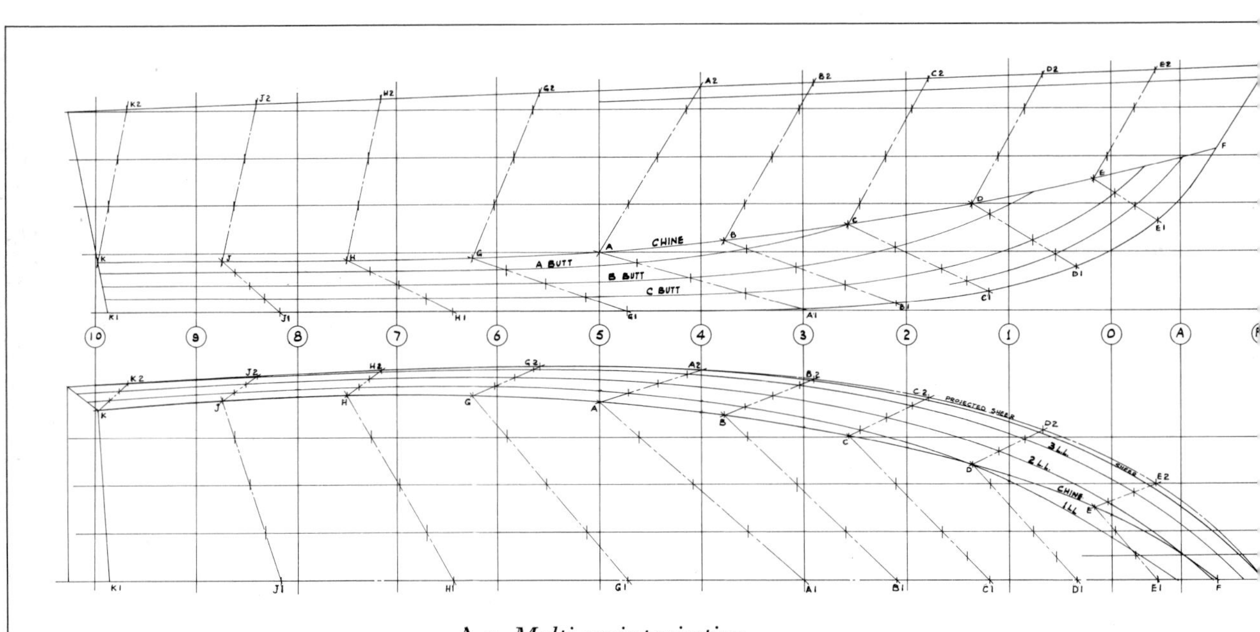

A-3 *Multi-conic projection.*

All designers will be familiar with the normal types of drawings that must necessarily be issued to the shop floor, to enable them to perform their function. One drawing that is sometimes overlooked, but is essential if the hull is to function at its maximum efficiency, is the shell expansion. This should indicate the precise location of all plate butts, giving dimensions from frames and bulkheads. These will, of course, not be located in areas of stress concentration. Stringer terminations should be shown where not continuous—i.e., when abutting a watertight or oiltight frame or bulkhead. Large scale details should indicate where scallops are positioned to enable welding to be continuous and avoid triaxial stresses (see figure A-2). Waterways should be shown clearly. It is very difficult to cut waterways—i.e., scallops in longitudinal and transverse framing to allow bilge water to drain to a point leading to a strum box, after the plating has been positioned. The type of welding; continuous, staggered intermittent, chain intermittent, and the length of weld and gap should be noted. Leg length and throat thickness of fillet welds and much other information should be laid out plainly. It is unfair to complain of sub-standards when no standards have been given.

Welding symbols are fully covered in British Standards, and no doubt in the Standards department of other countries, but unfortunately not all small yards are familiar with these expressions. This should be borne in mind when contemplating the general layout of all drawings. The purpose of a drawing is to elucidate, not confuse.

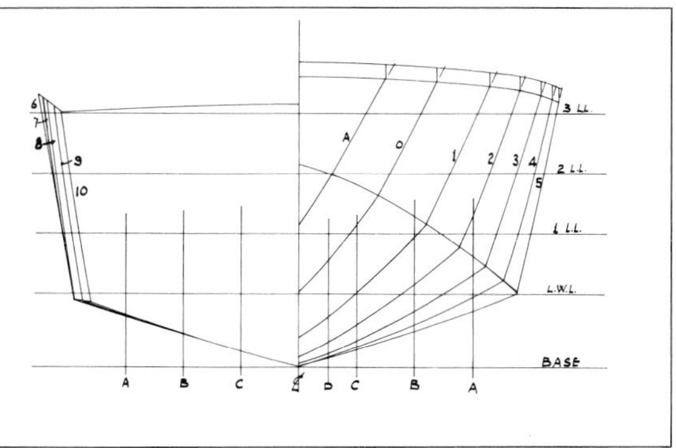

There are occasions when it may be considered advantageous to eliminate double curvature in hull plating. This can be achieved by using the multiconic method of hull design. This will not eliminate any of the normal functions necessary in the production of a general hull design. Its only purpose is to slightly modify some of the sections so that a hull plate will simply wrap around the hull, because compound curvature has been eliminated. Not all designers favour this method, because it does somewhat inhibit choice of shape. The method is particularly useful for the design of chine boats of moderate size. The various parts of the single sheet are laid out to bend suitably on cones of different ratios of height to diameter, and if properly laid out according to the principles of multi-conic projection, the edges of adjacent sheets will meet with a uniform welding gap. There are several methods by which the principle can be applied, and the method described is not the most exact, but it is very simple. The reason why this simple method can be used on aluminium is that aluminium, at least in the thinner gauges, will give a slight amount of double curvature naturally. Plywood will normally give no degree of double curvature, and so a different method of projection must be adopted using a common apex for the cone with all generators emanating from it, or from a secondary apex situated on one of the original generators.

To use our simplified multi-conic projection, the designer prepares his lines in the normal way, by drawing the profile and plan views. We now draw in the radians. It is probably easier to start with the midship section, and the first bottom radian is drawn to the first or second station position forward of this (figure A-3, p. 18). From the endings of the first radian, the chine, and keel to the chine, are divided into an equal number of parts, A to F and A′ to F. These points are then connected with additional radians B–B′, C–C′, D–D′, and E–E′. This equal spacing is for convenience only. From the profile these lines are projected to the plan below. Buttock lines are now drawn on the plan, and their intersections with the radians projected back to the profile. From these intersections the line of the buttocks may now be drawn. From the buttock heights in the profile, the shape of the bottom sections may be drawn in. (The aft body A to K is treated similarly.) To develop the topsides, the procedure is similar, but level lines are used instead of buttocks.

3 Tools and their Application

Cutting

Cutting of aluminium is normally carried out either by shearing or sawing. For straight cuts on material up to about 6 mm. thick, standard power guillotines produced for cutting up to 3 mm. thick steel are suitable. (See figure B-1).

Knife edges should be kept sharp, as blunt tools tend to burr the edges with such rather soft material. A clearance of one-tenth to one-eighth of the plate thickness is normal between top and bottom blade. Holding down pads on power guillotines produced for cutting steel should be changed for softer tips, usually of a plastic nature, as the harder type make indentations in the aluminium. This can usually be arranged with the supplier, and it is usually a simple matter to fit the softer pads in second-hand machinery. The power guillotine should have a length of cut slightly longer than the normal length of plate to be used; this would vary from 6 ft. to 12 ft. but the average length of bed is a little over 8 ft. and the average length of sheet and plate is 8 ft.

Hand or foot guillotines are used for shorter lengths and thinner gauges, up to about

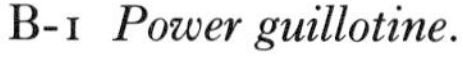

B-1 *Power guillotine.*

B-2 *Band saw.*

B-3 (centre) *Hand folder.*
B-4 (right) *Press brake.*

3 mm. Electric or air hand shears are very useful for sheet up to about 2 mm. particularly for intricate shapes. Nibblers, both machine and hand held portable, are used on plate up to about 6 mm. thick.

Band saws (see figure B-2), preferably with a deep throat, are used extensively over a wide range of thicknesses. A narrow blade of about $\frac{1}{2}$ in. wide is used for cutting shapes, and a blade about 1 in. wide for straight cuts. A skip tooth of about 8 teeth per in. is satisfactory for average thicknesses of 3 mm. to 6 mm. with slightly more T.P.I. for thinner sheets and less T.P.I. for thicker plates. Band saws should have a surface speed of 5,000 to 2,000 ft. per minute, with the slower speeds for the thicker plate.

If a variable speed saw is not available, the old fashioned heavy framed type used for cutting wood is quite suitable. For cutting straight parallel lines in any thickness plate, a circular saw, with carbide tipped blades, will provide an edge, that requires no further preparation for welding. Lubrication of the cutting edge with paraffin-oil mixture, or soluble oils, will improve the cutting efficiency and increase the blade life. Where cutting has to be made in situ, or in the centre of plates, a portable jig saw is very useful; different blades are available for use on a variety of materials.

Routers can be used for cutting the most intricate shapes on any thickness of plate. Where it is necessary partially to reduce the thickness of a plate, a router is essential. Templates have to be made, and the setting up time is really only justified if a number of similar items are to be produced. For batch production, time saving can be very significant. A water-soluble lubricant should be sprayed on to the cutter to prevent tool pick up and maintain the cutting edges.

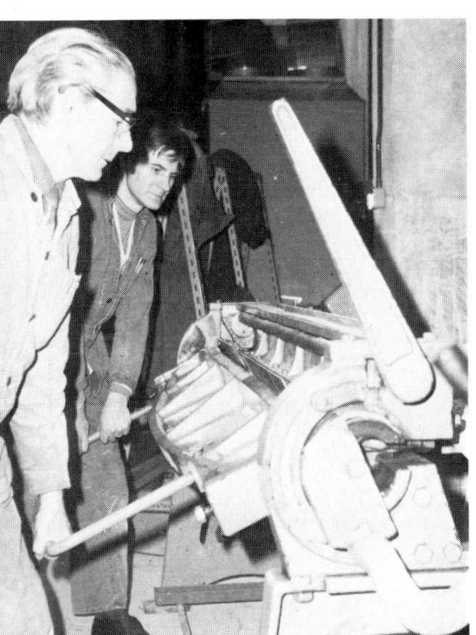

Forming

Straight line bending of thin material up to about 18 gauge can be dealt with by the hand folder, (see figure B-3) which is adequate and also simple to operate; for thicker materials of not too long a bend, a hand operated flypress of adequate size (about No. 6) is used. All other bending requires a press brake (see figure B-4), this should have at least an 8 ft. bed, and be capable of about 80 tons pressure. In the hands of a competent and resourceful operator, a wide variety of shapes can be produced with a minimum of tooling. A multi-vee block, and about three segmented bending knives, with say radii of $\frac{1}{8}$ in., $\frac{1}{4}$ in. and $\frac{3}{8}$ in. would be adequate for most bending jobs.

Wrappers—i.e., lengths of thin aluminium, bent around the knife edge, can be used for intermediate gauges. The knife selected for bending, would be dependent on the thickness of metal to be bent, and its hardness condition. Bend radii could vary from $\frac{1}{2}$T to 3T, (T=sheet thickness), whilst in practice, the material used in boat construction is fairly soft, usually O, or M, condition (see chapter 1), and $1\frac{1}{2}$T or 2T is normal. A certain amount of 'spring back' is to be expected, the actual amount can only be ascertained by experiment, so the punch or knife should have an included angle of about 86° where a 90° bend is required, to allow a slight overbend initially.

B-5 *Power rolls.*

B-6 (centre) *Planishing wheel.*
B-7 (right) *Shaping machine.*

Shaping

Cylindrical or conical shapes are produced on rolls, power or hand operated, depending on diameter of shape and thickness of material. It is normal to use power rolls (see figure B-5) for anything above about 16g, but if thicker materials are used on hand operated rolls it is probable that distortion of the rolls will occur.

There are normally three rolls arranged in pyramid fashion, with one fixed and the other two arranged variably, depending on thickness of material and diameter of shape to be produced.

A hand operated type with $3\frac{1}{2}$ in. diameter × 6 ft. rolls and a 6 in. diameter × 8 ft. rolls with 5 h.p. electric motor, would be found adequate for most boatyards. It is essential in all roll-forming that the surface of the rolls should be kept in a clean, polished condition, When not in use, they should be kept lightly oiled, and covered with protective paper. Before use, the oil, and any foreign matter must be removed. If pitting of the surface has occurred, protective paper should be used between the rolls and the workpiece.

Where double curvature is required in a plate, as in some skin panels, the planishing wheel is used (see figure B-6). The top wheel has a flat rim, and the lower is shaped, depending on the curvature required. The workpiece is fed between the wheels to the area that requires shaping, then the lower wheel is raised so that the workpiece is under pressure and the workpiece is moved back and forth through this pressure area. This has the effect of thinning the metal locally and thickening it on the perimeter, which means that the centre of the panel has been stretched; the result is that the panel will have 'belly'. A degree of skill is required in this operation, which will come with

practice; it is very much easier to put shape into a panel than to remove it, so a cautious approach is needed, with constant reference to the final shape, either the job itself or templates.

To shape extrusions or plate, a tool is needed with top and bottom jaws which grip the workpiece, and with movable sections in the jaws, which can either press together laterally or press apart; these have the effect of shrinking or stretching the perimeter of the workpiece, which in turn produces an inside or outside curve. These machines are made in various sizes, depending on the gauge and size of extrusion to be treated. The smallest for use on up to about 1 mm. can be used in the fly press, the largest can accommodate thicknesses of up to about 6 mm. (see figure B-7). Skills for operating these machines are quickly acquired, and some very complicated shapes can be produced, very quickly.

A certain amount of hand planishing or beating will inevitably be required. Wooden mallets, pear shaped and round headed have their particular uses, and are used over a metal stake. This is sometimes referred to as raising. Mallets are usually made of box wood, but rawhide, leather, fibre, rubber and metal hammers all have their uses. Tools and workpiece should always be kept clean and smooth as the soft metal is easily scratched. The grades of aluminium used in boatbuilding are usually of the work-hardening type, so the material should not be overworked. The number of blows should be kept to the minimum, to avoid excessive hardening and cracking.

Aluminium generally is very ductile, and with the correct tooling, a little practice, and gentle persuasion, will respond very readily to intelligently applied working.

Hand power tools

In the very small boatyard, employing less than six on the shop floor, the ordinary electric drills etc. commonly used for wood construction, should prove adequate. Where more than this are employed, a compressed air system which offers the use of pneumatic tools should be considered. Once installed, the savings are considerable, and a large variety of tools can be served.

Where tools are to be used continuously, small electric motors suffer very badly, whereas air tools have very few moving parts, and require far less maintenance. A compressor of adequate size must be installed, with power to spare for expansion. Particular care must be given to the layout of the installation, so that moisture, inevitably produced from the air during compression, is removed from the pipe line immediately before the air enters the tool, and at the same juncture oil is introduced into the line. This is accomplished by fitting filters and lubricators and has the effect of reducing corrosion, and lubricating moving parts automatically.

Pneumatic drills of up to $\frac{1}{4}$ in. diameter capacity would normally have an operating speed of around 5,000 rpm, thus greatly reducing drilling time over electric drills.

Metal remover

Edge preparation for welding (see chapter 4) sometimes makes it necessary to remove a portion of the inside faces of the butt joint, depending on the thickness of plate to be joined, to permit good penetration. For this purpose use a carbide edge cutter with guides either side, set on a mandrel which fits into a chuck or collet of a portable pneumatic tool, capable of about 25,000 rpm (see figure B-8). Where more than one pass is required in a welded joint or where repairs are called for, it is necessary to chip back to sound metal. This is very effectively and quickly carried out by fitting the air tool with a v-cutter that mills grooves in the weld metal (see figure B-9). Metal removing burrs are also used in the same air tool; these have a variety of uses, and are available in many shapes (see figure B-10).

Rivet guns

Two general types of riveting tools are used; one is the reciprocating hammer type, for use on solid rivets, where the rivet is entered from one side of the hole, a dolly is held under the head and the tail is burred over with the vibrating punch; the other is the 'pop' rivet gun, where the rivet is entered from the same side as the gun is operated, an extended mandrel in the rivet is gripped and pulled, and when the rivet is secured in place, the mandrel breaks off. Both types of tool are air operated, and each type of rivet serves a particular function (see chapter 5).

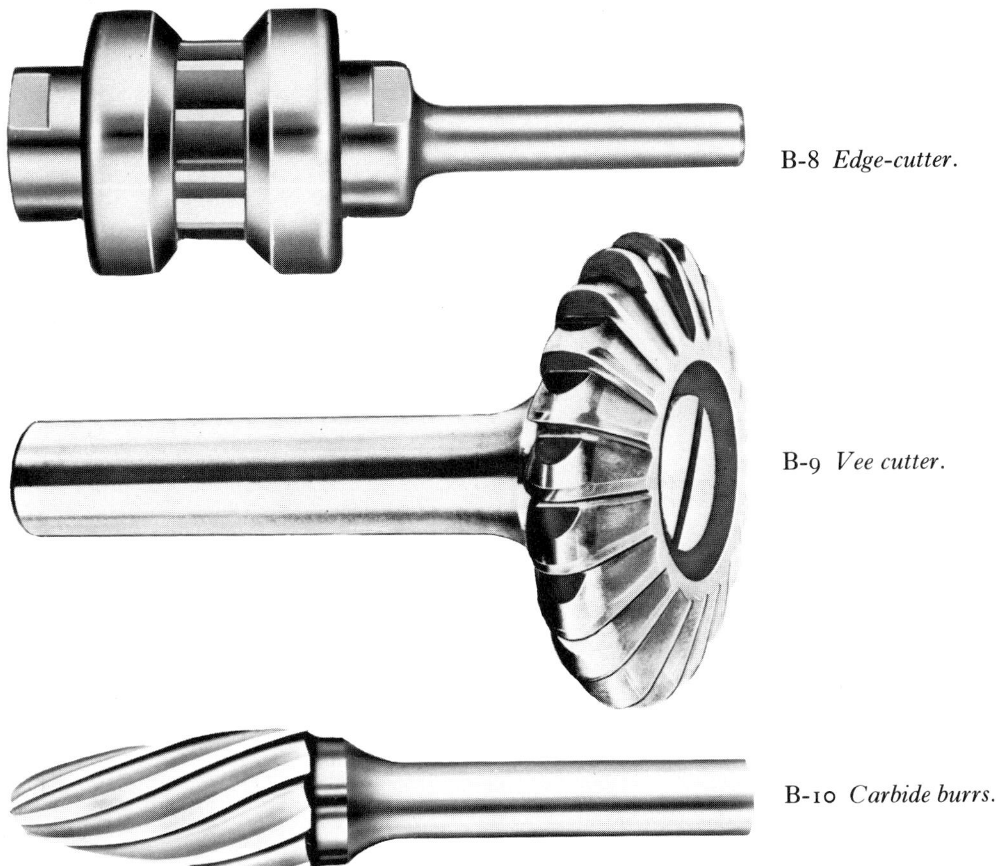

B-8 *Edge-cutter.*

B-9 *Vee cutter.*

B-10 *Carbide burrs.*

Grinding

The standard type of carborundum wheel is not suitable for use with aluminium, which is rather soft so quickly clogs and renders the wheel useless. The most satisfactory results are obtained with the use of special discs spinning at between 12,000 and 15,000 rpm when fitted onto portable air tools. The discs are produced in various grades of grit, and are flexible (soft) types or rigid (hard). Great care must be exercised, especially with the hard disc, not to dig the edges into the material, thereby causing ridges which would be very difficult to eliminate.

Grinding is normally used for metal removal on edges and excess welding. For strength reasons butt joints on the skin should not be ground down flush, but a small weld bead should be left proud of the surface. The only exceptions would be where the owner demands, for appearance sake, or on the bottom of planing hulls, where a smooth surface to obtain planing speeds is essential.

For finishing prior to painting, linishers or vibratory sanders are used; some of these are fitted with water feeds so that sanding paper of the wet and dry variety can be used, which increases the efficiency by reducing the tendency to clog.

4 Welding

Only two methods of welding will be considered. M.I.G. (Metal inert gas) and T.I.G. (Tungsten inert gas). Oxy-acetylene and metal-arc welding are not recommended for the magnesium alloys normally used in boat construction, because of the poor joint efficiencies, resulting in lower mechanical properties and corrosion problems.

Selection of process

The selection of T.I.G. or M.I.G. for any particular type of joint or weld depends on many factors. The most important being the following:

Parent metal thickness

This is described in more detail under the various process headings.

The appearance

The finished joint depends largely upon the quality of the pre-weld preparation and the skill of the welder, but under equal conditions T.I.G. is capable of producing a better looking weld than M.I.G.

Economy

Where high production is called for, M.I.G. is normally more economical than T.I.G. However, the quantity of welding will affect not only the selection of process, but also the choice between the manual and mechanised version of these processes.

Distortion
In general, M.I.G. with its lower overall heat input, creates fewer distortion problems than T.I.G. The introduction of mechanised welding can also considerably lessen the problem.

Access
The type of equipment will largely depend on the accessibility to the joint area. T.I.G. equipment is less bulky, and the rate of deposition of filler wire is more easily controlled.

The T.I.G. process
In the T.I.G. process an A.C. arc is struck between a non-consumable tungsten electrode and the workpiece, the filler rod being fed independently. Fluxes are unnecessary as the arc itself cleans the electrode and weld pool, whilst re-oxidation is prevented by a shield of inert argon gas which envelops the area. Control by the welder of both heat input and the wire feed makes possible, in turn, a control of penetration which is normally unobtainable with manual unbacked M.I.G. welding. The T.I.G. process is, therefore, normally favoured for un-backed butt joints which are only accessible from one side. Similarly, such precise manual control is an advantage where the weld path is complex. Welds to Class I standards and of the best appearance can easily be made with this process.

Manual T.I.G. welding speeds vary from 12.7 to 63.5 cm. per minute. It is possible with advantage to combine the M.I.G. and T.I.G. processes. For instance, where a butt joint has to be welded, access is possible from one side only, and a backing bar cannot be fitted. A root pass could be laid down with T.I.G. and subsequent passes depending on thickness of parent metal, could be made with the M.I.G. process.

T.I.G. equipment
A.C. or D.C. units may be used. A composite unit which includes all the necessary auxiliaries is usually used for T.I.G. welding of aluminium. However, a conventional A.C. transformer of suitable current capacity, and having a minimum open circuit voltage of 70 v., may be used if connected in series with a separate H.F. unit, a D.C. suppressor, and a contactor as auxiliary equipment. An H.F. (high frequency) or

surge injector unit is necessary for the arc to be struck between the electrode and workpiece without 'touching down' which would contaminate the joint with tungsten and the electrode with aluminium. Should this happen, the tungsten-contaminated area must be chipped out and the electrode cleaned by grinding, before welding can be continued. A D.C. suppressor is necessary to give the required balanced current wave-form, which in turn will facilitate welding and improve weld quality.

The presence of a contactor in the electrical circuit is essential for safety reasons. Because aluminium welding uses higher open circuit voltages than steel, the supply must be disconnected immediately the arc is broken. The contactor does this automatically.

T.I.G. torches

Torches for low-duty welding applications, up to about 100 A., are normally air-cooled, but for high duty cycles or greater currents, water-cooling is necessary.

T.I.G. electrodes

To minimise weld contamination, pure or zirconiated tungsten electrodes are preferable to the thoriated type. Also, they have slightly higher current ratings and in general give rise to a more stable arc.

T.I.G. filler rods

T.I.G. filler rod is supplied in straight lengths in various sizes. Rods must be of good quality and it is essential that they be cleaned before welding if they are supplied in the 'as drawn' condition when there is no subsequent cleaning by the manufacturer. This may be done with emery cloth. Colour coding on the tips indicate the filler alloy. Each manufacturer determines his own coding. Where the parent material is unknown, a cutting from the parent material may be used as filler rod.

Gas shield

Argon gas of welding quality, having a minimum purity of 99.95%, may be used for all aluminium welding, particularly for thin gauges.

Helium may be used, and is especially useful for thick gauges, where a faster arc travel speed can be attained. It also requires less edge preparation, and a higher quality weld can result, due to less porosity. Where a butt weld is made with passes on each side of the plate, the width of the overlap between the two weld passes is about three times greater for helium than argon. This allows a greater degree of latitude for misalignment between passes due to tracking errors.

Helium requires different gas shielding conditions, and a different welding technique, than when using argon. Outside of the U.S.A., helium is generally much more expensive, and difficult to obtain than argon, and for that reason is little used.

Fault finding of contaminated welds—T.I.G.

The following items can be responsible for contaminated welds:

1. Too much or not enough gas
2. Incorrect torch angle
3. Size of ceramic gas shield
4. Too high a current
5. Welding in draughty conditions
6. Cleanliness of materials
7. Using incorrect current (A.C./D.C.)
8. Wet or greasy plate
9. Electrode too far out
10. Arc length too long
11. (A.C. only) welding without suppressor
12. Incorrect filler wires

The M.I.G. process

In the M.I.G. process, an arc is struck between the workpiece and a continuously fed aluminium wire which acts as both the filler and the electrode. Fluxes are unnecessary. The arc itself cleans the electrode and weld pool whilst re-oxidation is prevented by a shield of inert gas, either argon or helium, which envelops the area. The filler wire feed is semi-automatic; wire is fed mechanically from the gun into the weld pool at a speed balancing the rate of burn-off, which in turn is determined by the current setting required for the weld. The arc is sufficiently self-adjusting for small movements of the torch etc. to be accommodated. A controlled arc system will be found to give additional control. Penetration cannot generally be controlled as closely as is possible in T.I.G. welding so butt joints must be backed, or welded from both sides of the joint, except where pulsed arc is used. For manual welding, the spool of filler wire is mounted either separately on a wire feed unit ('ten pound' M.I.G.) or on the torch itself ('one pound' M.I.G.), the latter arrangement making for exceptional torch mobility and is especially useful for tacking. The small diameter of the wire (nominally 1.2 or 1.6 mm.) makes possible a high current density, giving deep penetration, and welding speeds appreciably higher than those possible in T.I.G. welding; consequently with less total heat input, distortion is less likely. Manual welding speeds range from 33 to 140 cm. per minute.

M.I.G. welding is generally carried out with the torch held in the hand, and with the wire being fed automatically at a controlled speed, distortion is reduced to a minimum. When a mechanised set-up is used, the arc length, rate of wire feed, and movement of torch are all controlled, the resultant of which is usually a far better weld, both mechanically and in appearance. The different M.I.G. welding processes are identified by the manner of filler wire transfer.

Dip transfer

Can be used successfully in down hand, vertical and overhead positions. As the name infers, filler wire is transferred by the tip 'dipping' into the weld pool. More generally used for welding sheet up to about $\frac{3}{16}$ in. thick (5 mm.) or tacking heavier plate in position prior to fully welding.

Spray transfer

Used principally for down hand welding of plate thicknesses greater than $\frac{1}{4}$ in. (6 mm.). The metal is sprayed from the wire tip in a continuous stream of small droplets to the weld pool.

More expertise is needed on the part of the welder to control the weld pool from 'spilling over' on vertical or overhead runs.

Pulsed transfer

Pulsed arc welding is a form of spray transfer, but because lower currents are used, the welder has a greater degree of control of the weld pool. There are essentially two integrated power sources. One 'side' maintains the tip of the wire molten, whilst the other side transfers the droplets into the weld pool. Pulsed transfer is a newer and more sophisticated method of welding. It demands a greater degree of skill and expertise, and bridges the gap between, and extends into the ranges of dip and spray transfer. Down hand, vertical, and overhead welding to a high standard is possible.

Preparation for welding

Before welding can commence, two conditions must exist. There must be a good set-up of the material to be welded, and the weld area must be clean.

All aluminium alloys of the type used in boat construction are covered with a hard tenacious oxide film. It is this natural covering that gives aluminium its corrosion resistance. If the film is removed by chemical or mechanical means, it starts to re-form almost immediately. Whilst this oxide film is valuable in providing the corrosion resistance of aluminium, it interferes with the welding process and must be removed before or during welding. The melting point of the oxide film is about 2020°C. The melting point of pure aluminium is about 650°C. Therefore, the temperature differential will allow the aluminium to melt before the oxide film. To some extent the oxide is removed by the arc during welding and the inert gas shield prevents its re-forming. A superior weld will result if the oxide film is broken up immediately prior to welding. This can be done quite simply, by wire brushing the area, preferably with a stainless steel wire brush. An ordinary brush can be used, but tends to contaminate the weld. The brushes should be kept clean and only used for this operation. They should also be changed frequently.

Edge preparation

On butt joints of about $\frac{1}{4}$ in. thick plate and thicker, it is necessary to taper a portion of the inside faces of the joint to allow greater penetration. This is best achieved by using a carbide edge cutter metal remover, as described under chapter 3 on tooling, or a planing machine, or even a dreadnought file, provided great care is taken to ensure a straight and even taper. Fig. C-1 p. 34 indicates the general form necessary. Manufacturers of aluminium sheet and welding machines distribute to their customers quite freely excellent booklets covering the requirements for edge preparation for all types of joints. Experiments should be carried out using these tables, and where successful proceeded with. As experience is gained, some welders may produce better results, with slight variations. This is to be expected as no two welders weld precisely alike, and each should develop his own technique.

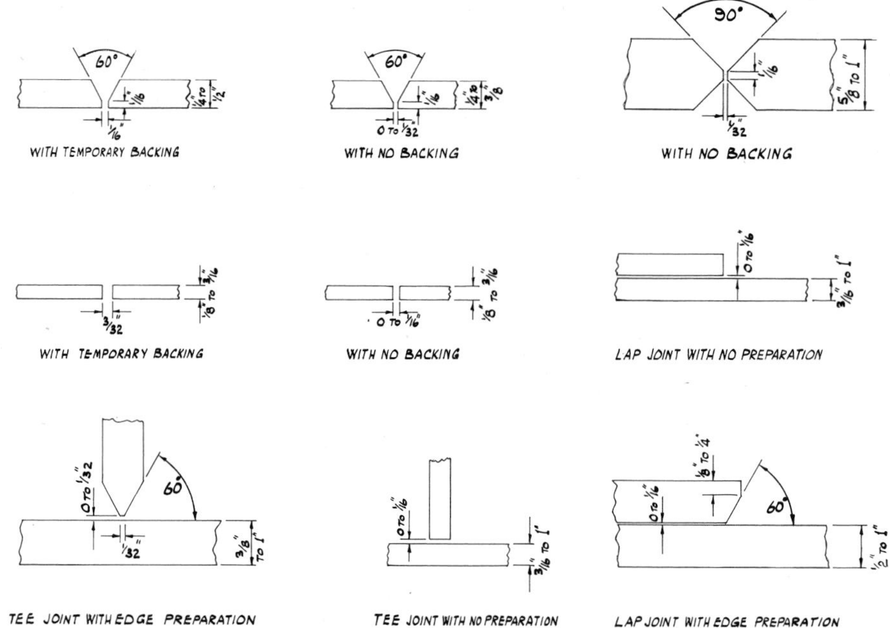

C-1 *Edge preparation.*

Cleanliness

The need for cleanliness in the weld zone and a little beyond cannot be stressed too highly. Contaminates trapped in the weld pool will cause porosity, which will inevitably affect the mechanical properties of the weld. All dirt, moisture, grease etc., should be removed with a de-greasing agent, that will evaporate fairly quickly, such as white spirit, or acetone. Cleaning swabs of a non-fluffy material should be changed frequently. Cleaning should be carried out immediately prior to welding. The storage area should be clean and dry, sheets should be stood on edge, preferably on wood battens, not too tightly packed, with a good air circulation.

Welding machines

There is at the moment a great proliferation of welding equipment, available from many countries. Very careful consideration should be given before deciding on the choice of a particular type or manufacturer. Cost, although important, is not the prime consideration. A piece of equipment that does not fully satisfy your requirements can be expensive at any price. Future possible needs, as well as present commitments, should be considered. Some machines perform a variety of tasks: dip, spray, and pulsed arc for instance, but it is only one machine, and only one operator can use it at a time. If that machine is out of commission, all welding ceases. It may be advantageous to operate a machine for each of these tasks separately. A minimum requirement would be T.I.G.; preferably with a water-cooled torch, for light gauge, tube, complex weld path, repairs etc., a small M.I.G. set, with air-cooled torch, up to about 200 A., for all light gauge work, positional welding, tacking etc., and a heavier M.I.G. set with water-cooled torch capable of about 350 amps. that can be used for heavier wire and longer runs. When using water-cooled torches with water from mains supply, a pressure-reducing valve should be incorporated, otherwise after a very short time, leaking joints will be a constant source of annoyance. An alternative is to fit a self-contained circulating system incorporating a small lift pump and tank. When deciding the choice of manufacturer, after-sales service, and spares supply, should be considered. T.I.G. units are comparatively simple machines and seldom give trouble. M.I.G. units are far more complex, and constant electrical maintenance is advisable to ensure trouble-free operation, and minimal down time. Some welding plant manufacturers offer training facilities. These are well worth attendance by new operators. It is no longer considered sufficient to merely stand alongside another operator to learn the craft. Most operators have some bad habits and these are easier to learn than eradicate. There is no substitute for practical instruction from a skilled demonstrator. Many manufacturers also spend considerable effort developing new techniques. It is sensible to take advantage of these offers.

Fully automatic welding

There are many advantages to be gained by the mechanisation of the M.I.G. process. These are, higher welding speeds, less distortion, and generally better welds due to controlled arc length and rate of travel. Pipe welding machines are used extensively where a high work through-put is required, but the capital cost would seldom be justified by the boatbuilder.

Plate welding machines for straight line butts can very quickly pay for themselves in time saved both in the initial welding, and by eliminating to a large extent the need for repairs, to an inferior weld. There are two types of plate welding machine. The first where the workpiece is brought to the machine, the second where the machine is taken to the workpiece. The former consists of a metal beam to which the plates are clamped, and an overhead carriage that carries the M.I.G. torch. This type is normally restricted to a flat, straight weld path. The latter type, manufactured

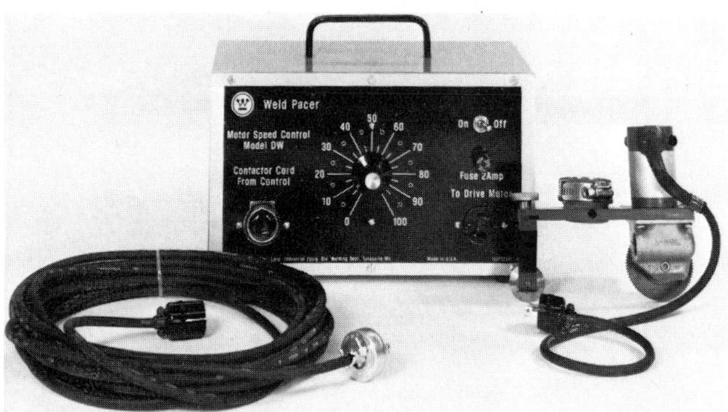

C-2 *Automatic M.I.G. Weld Pacer.*

by a large American company, is marketed as a 'Weld Pacer' (see figure C-2), and consists of a small platform to which a M.I.G. gun barrel fits through the collet in the drive unit. Two guide wheels, one providing traction, travel in the v-butt joint. The angle of the gun to the workpiece can be varied according to the collet securing the gun to the carriage, and the arc length is determined by the length of barrel protruding through the collet. The traction wheel speed is variable, as is the wire feed. Once all the variables have been set, after trial runs, the quality of all welds will be similar. The great advantage of the weld pacer is that it can be used on the bench, or on the boat hull, following a contour. Where long runs, or high amperages are called for, a water-cooled torch should be considered.

Multi-pass welds

More than one-pass welds may be necessary in plate of $\frac{1}{4}$ in. thick (6 mm.) and over, particularly where manual as opposed to machine welding is employed. Before a weld is laid on top of another, it is necessary to remove the dross formed by the initial bead. This function is performed by backchipping with the pneumatic tool fitted with a v-cutter mentioned in chapter 2 (see figure B-8). It is readily seen when sound metal is exposed.

Plasma-arc

Plasma-arc welding and cutting is essentially an extension of the T.I.G. process, using a mixture of argon and hydrogen gases. This welding process is claimed to improve the quality of the weld, with a greater tolerance of varying arc length, a greater degree of weld penetration, higher welding speeds, and reduced risk of electrode contamination. The rate of distortion is also reduced, due to the narrow plasma arc, reducing the width of the heatspread to the workpiece.

Plasma cutting is a very efficient method of cutting most metals up to about 1 in. thick (25 mm.), including stainless steel. A good clean edge results, requiring very little attention for a weld preparation finish. The cutting agent is a high speed jet of gas, heated to temperatures up to 30,000°F by an electric arc.

These are rather specialist pieces of equipment, and although very useful for their own particular jobs, would hardly justify the capital expense for many yards.

Run on-run off plates

These are extra pieces of parent metal tacked to the beginning and ending of the weld joint. They are particularly useful where no trimming allowance is possible. When starting a weld, a little time is taken to achieve full penetration, and at the termination a crater is formed. It is better that these deficiencies should occur on waste material, that is later removed.

Backing bars

Where a M.I.G. butt weld is to be used and the back of the weld is accessible it is usual to fit a backing bar. The value of this backing is that it prevents the force of the M.I.G. arc from blowing through the joint. Where edge preparation is provided, and a small gap is made at the root of the joint, full penetration can be assured. A backing bar can take one of two forms, permanent or temporary. Permanent backers are strips similar to the parent metal, welded to the back of the joint. It is necessary to fuse the two edges of the joint to the backing strip, so a root opening greater than that used with a temporary backer should be allowed (see figure C-3).

Temporary backers are usually of steel or stainless steel and are grooved to allow an underbead of metal to protrude below the joint. This ensures full penetration. The groove may be quite shallow between $\frac{1}{32}$ in. and $\frac{1}{16}$ in. deep, and wide enough not to restrict the edges of the bead. The shape of the groove is usually rounded, but it may be rectangular (see figure C-4). The area of the joint must be well secured to the backing bar by clamping, or bolting.

C-3 *Permanent backers.*

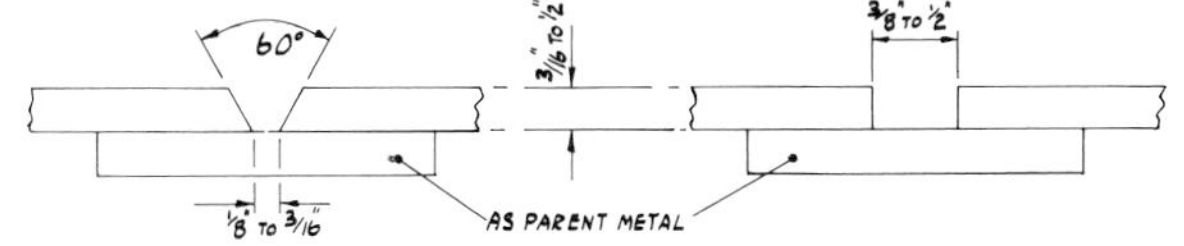

C-4 *Temporary backer.*

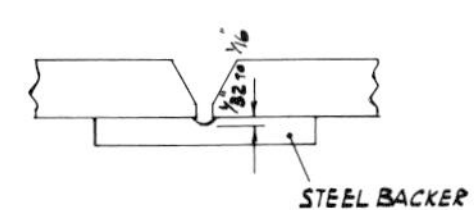

Control of distortion

Welding distortion is a result of localised heating and cooling. Expansion and contraction of metal in the weld zone, whilst being constrained by the surrounding metal causes deformation and built in stresses. Many factors contribute as to how much, and how serious, these are, and what should be done to reduce or correct the effects.

The four types of distortion to be found in welded joints are illustrated in figure C-6. They are: (1) angular distortion, (2) shrinkage across the weld, (3) longitudinal distortion, (4) throat shrinkage. Of these, number 4 has so little effect it can be ignored.

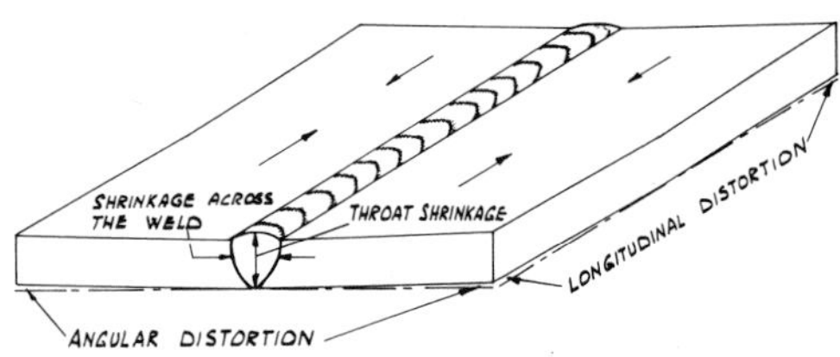

C-5 *Types of plate distortion.*

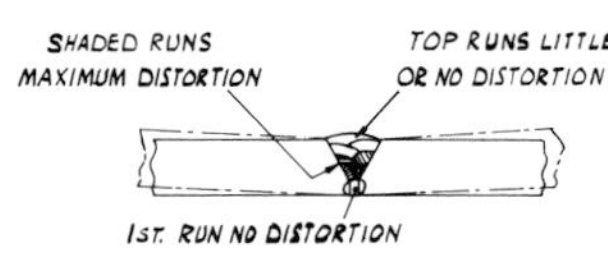

C-6 *Single Vee'd butt weld.*

Angular distortion may be illustrated by a multi-run butt weld (see figure C-7). Provided that the joint is not too rigidly held, the contraction of the first run will merely draw the plates together, without causing distortion. The succeeded runs will tend to cause distortion, as the first run will attempt to resist the contraction of these subsequent runs, which by their combined contraction stresses, create a superior force which tends to lift the edges of the plates in an upward direction. The top runs will have little effect on the amount of distortion caused, as by the time they are deposited the preceding runs are sufficient to provide an anchor against the contraction stresses exerted by the top runs.

In the welding a single run vee'd butt weld, the resulting distortion will also tend to force the plate edges in an upward direction, due to the higher contraction stresses imposed by the larger amount of heated weld metal at the top of the vee.

For welding thicker plates, a double vee'd joint preparation is recommended (see figure C-7). If the runs of welding are deposited in the upper and lower vee's alternately, the tendency towards distortion caused by the contraction of the welds in the upper vee is counteracted to a large extent by the opposing contraction stresses in the lower runs.

The angular distortion described for butt welds is also possible in a fillet welded joint. Figure C-8 indicates this. As in the case of buttwelded joints, the greater the number of runs employed, the greater could be the distortion. To minimise the effect of angular distortion, the following procedures should be considered, and the appropriate action take; rigid jigging, pre-setting, balancing of stresses by welding from both sides. Where distortion has occurred, straighten mechanically.

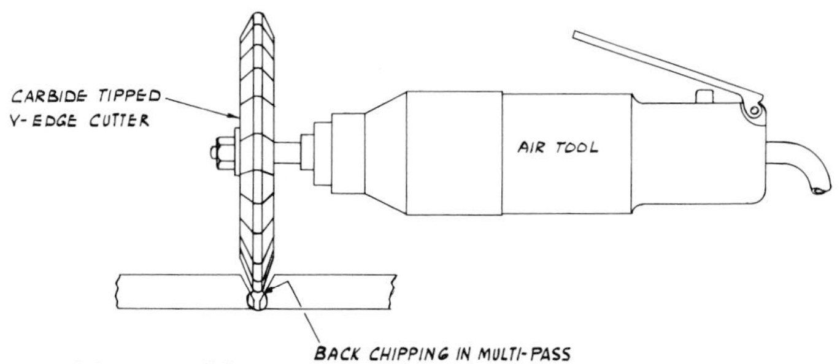

C-7 *Back chipping in multi-pass welds.*

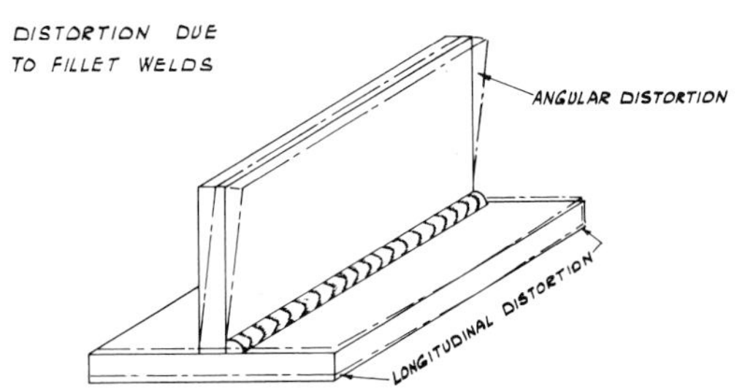

C-8 *Distortion to fillet weld.*

Longitudinal distortion results from longitudinal contraction of the weld. If there is sufficient trimming allowance, this may not be too troublesome. If contraction of the weld is critical, the following could minimise the effect; high welding speeds, back step sequences, multiple weld beads, and rigid jigging. To correct the problem, mechanically stretch the weld area, starting from the centre.

Shrinkage across the weld is caused by transverse contraction of the weld. To minimise, use rigid jigging, high welding speeds, minimum edge preparation.

The following general rules should be considered at the outset to minimise distortion problems:

(1) Keep the amount of welding to a minimum. Joints can sometimes be eliminated by using formed or extruded sections. Butt welds should use a minimum of edge preparation and root opening. All weld sizes should be kept as small as strength will allow.

(2) Use intermittent welds rather than continuous ones. All other considerations being equal.

(3) Use methods and conditions which give the highest welding speeds—e.g., M.I.G. welding, machine welding, flat position welding.

(4) Use jigging where appropriate.

(5) Position joints where they will cause least distortion—e.g., at or close to, neutral axes, or position so that weld contraction stresses tend to balance each other.

(6) Use a welding sequence that will balance out the stresses.

(7) After experiment to determine amount, pre-set members, so that when distortion does occur it will result in an acceptable finish.

A simple illustration of distortion is that of two flat plates joined by a single run buttweld. During the progress of welding, the free ends of the plate butt will either open out, or close up in front of the weld unless precautions are taken. If a small electrode, slow speed and low current are employed, during welding, there will be, on each side of the joint, a comparatively small heat area expanding and a considerably larger area which is cooling and contracting. The contraction area, therefore, exerts the superior force, and the plates tend to draw together in front of the weld. Conversely, if large gauge electrodes, high welding speed and high currents are used, then there will be a large area of expending metal and a much smaller area of contraction. Thus the expansion area exerts the superior force and the plates will open out in front of the weld as it progresses.

These and other forms of distortion may be kept within reasonable limits by means of wedging, tacking or clamping. If the plates tend to draw together as the weld progresses, the gap may be uniformly maintained by inserting a wedge into the open end and removing it when the welding approaches the end of the joint. When the plates tend to open out in front of the weld, the remedy is simple. By tack welding

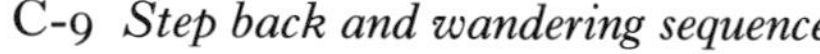
C-9 *Step back and wandering sequence.*

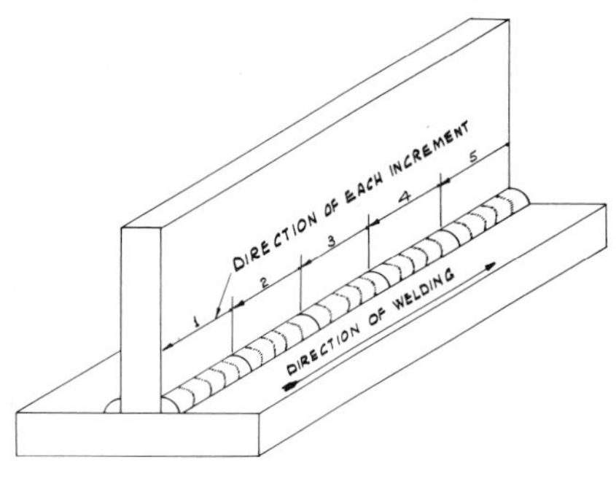

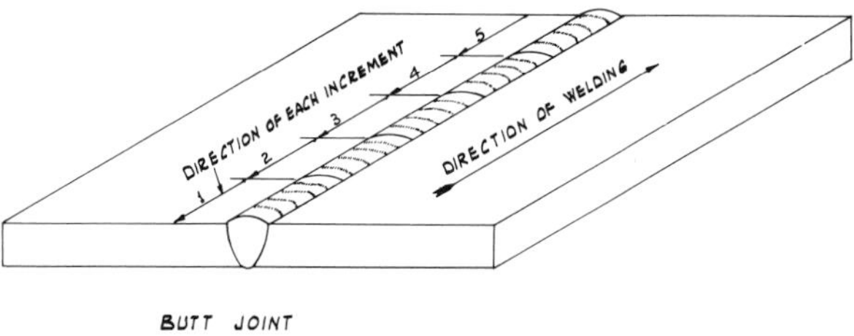

STEP BACK SEQUENCE

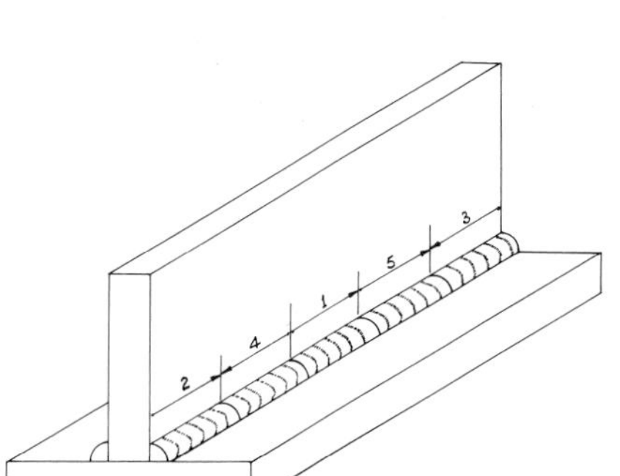

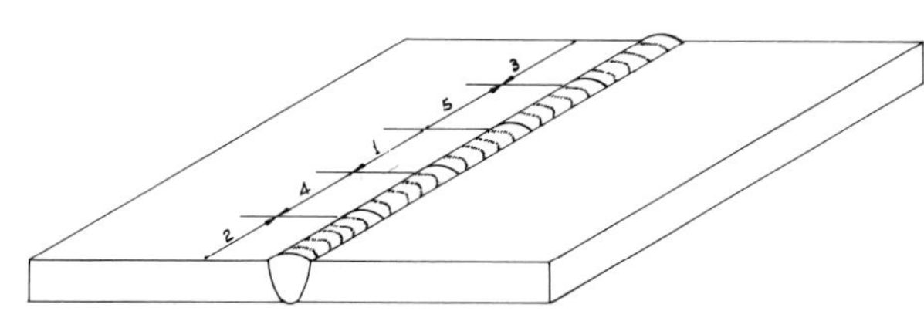

WANDERING SEQUENCE

the plates at intervals along the joint, sufficient restraint is imposed to overcome the tendency of the gap to widen. Alternatively, either case may be dealt with by efficiently clamping the joint to prohibit excessive movement of the plates during welding.

Where the avoidance of distortion is of paramount importance, the use of a welding sequence may assist. The two types of sequence most generally employed are the 'stepback' and the 'wandering' sequence, both of which are illustrated in figure C-9. In the stepback sequence, the increments of welding are deposited individually in a direction opposite to that in which the welding is progressing—i.e., in welding from left to right, each short run of weld metal is deposited working from right to left so that each increment stops where the previous one started.

A wandering sequence is adopted by depositing the first increment at mid length of the joint, and arranging the succeeding runs in a numbered sequence and a symmetrical pattern on each side of the first. No set order is necessary for these 'staggered' deposits, providing always that each increment is arranged as far as possible from the preceding one.

A good deal of space has been devoted to the subject of distortion, not because it is usually a major problem (it is less of a problem with the non heat-treatable magnesium type alloys in the 'O' or 'M' condition, due to their high ductility quality, than with the heat-treatable alloys, and a great deal less of a problem than with steel), but if the operator is aware of the internal struggle that is going on within the structure of the metal, many of the mysteries, and frustrations, will be the more easily understood and counter measures put into effect. No hard and fast rules can be laid down about the control of distortion, because there are so many variable factors that influence the effect. As the operator gains experience through experiment and useful work, a background of knowledge will be accumulated to combat and minimise a possible problem.

Jigging

Jigs are tools used to locate and hold in position parts that are being worked upon. They can range from a welding tack, to a revolving boat jig that allows the whole vessel to be rolled over to any position. The number of times a jig will be used may well determine its complexity.

Properly designed jigs provide means for the easy handling of the work and for accurately aligning the edges to be joined. Thus making greater production economy and precision. Jig design should aim at simplicity. Some typical welding jigs are shown in figure 10, page 42.

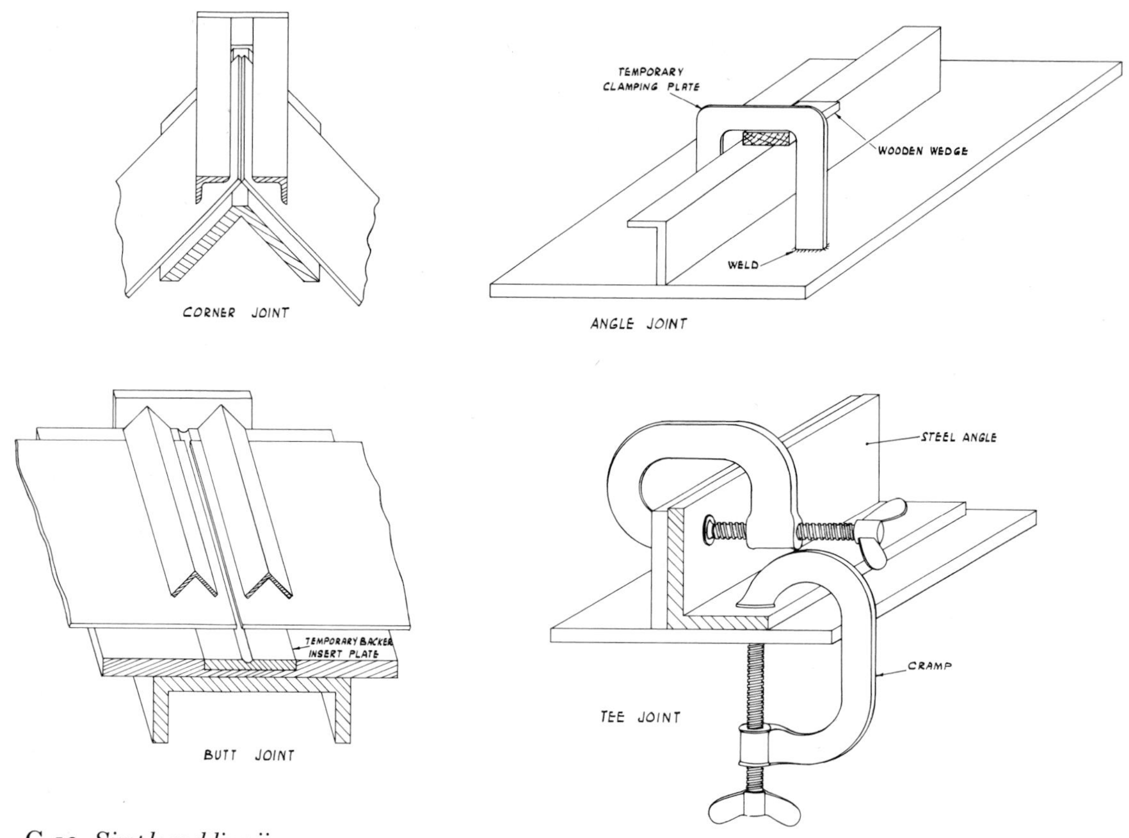

C-10 *Simple welding jigs.*

Weld faults

The tensile strength even of sound welds varies appreciably owing to the effects of joint preparation and method of welding. Not all welds are sound ones, and defects are very often present. The effect these have on weld strength and hence on commercial acceptance is, however, mostly a matter of guesswork. Very often welds are rejected simply because the inspection method picks out one particular defect such as porosity very well, but with little regard to its influence on mechanical properties. Accurate knowledge is, therefore, required of the influence of both the size and distribution of defects on weld strengths, so that acceptance or rejection can be based on realistic standards. There are as yet no published standards whereby to assess the influence of these defects on weld performance. Investigations are being carried out in various laboratories, and it is to be hoped these findings will be published and in time lead to accepted standards.

Common defects and their causes

Defects in aluminium welds result principally from faulty welding technique or from bad preparation of joints. They may be dealt with in five groups, each of which can be subdivided. Almost all have an adverse effect on strength particularly in fatigue.

Cracking

The most common type of cracking in aluminium welds is longitudinal, occurring along the centre or along the edge of the weld bead. The cause is usually a combination of two factors; susceptibility to hot shortness, and development of restraining stresses. Cracks on the centre of a weld are usually associated with hot shortness in the weld metal, and those at the edge with hot shortness of the parent metal. Both are more likely to occur with a welding technique which produces a large molten weld pool. Hot shortness is purely a function of composition and to counteract it filler alloys are used which give welds as far removed from the peak cracking composition as possible.

Restraining stresses may be set up by incorrect welding sequences or poor jigging. Both of these can cause cracking. Furthermore, shrinkage of solidifying weld metal under restraint at the end of the weld run may cause crater cracking. This can be avoided by filling the crater with additional metal before the arc is broken, or, in automatic welding, by increasing speed and reducing current shortly before the arc is extinguished. Occasionally, crater cracks in a previous pass are not completely repaired by subsequent passes, and the defective areas then have to be chipped out and re-welded. In welding required to be fluid-tight, crater cracks are possible sites for leakage.

Weld cracks often undetectable by radiography can result from relative movement between the parent metal surfaces whilst the weld pool is only partially solidified. Such movement may be caused by spring back, by poor jigging, or by distortion due to heat.

Transverse cracking is a comparatively rare defect and only occurs under conditions of longitudinal constraint such as are associated with frequent stops and starts or with severe changes in welding speed.

Lack of fusion

Lack of fusion is invariably due either to insufficient current, to misalignment, or to poor preparation which leaves oxide films or oil on the surfaces to be joined. It can be classified into three readily distinguishable types illustrated in figure C-11. The first type is lack of penetration, a serious defect resulting from using insufficient current to

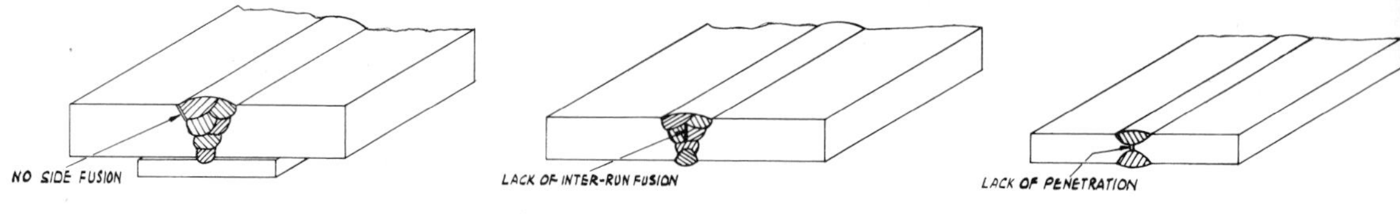

C-11 *Lack of fusion.*

melt the full joint thickness. In single-pass welds, the bottom (root) surfaces are not melted and a sharp open notch is left. In multi-pass (welded from both sides), the depth of fusion is insufficient to penetrate the opposite weld and an unjoined gap is left in the middle, causing a sharp internal notch.

The second type is lack of inter-run fusion, which occasionally occurs in multi-pass welds. Despite adequate penetration which re-melts the preceding pass, proper interfusion of the succeeding one is prevented by oxide, dirt, or oil.

The third type, lack of side fusion, which occurs in T.I.G. welds and in M.I.G. welds in thick plate, is due to misalignment of the weld torch, to insufficient current, or to oxide on the parent metal edges, so that the parent metal is only partially fused during welding.

Poor weld shape

A properly shaped weld provides enough build-up to counteract the lower properties of the cast weld-metal, whilst at the same time presenting a smooth profile without stress raising notches. Common defects in weld shape are illustrated in figure C-13.

Undercutting is reduction in thickness below that of the parent metal; it is caused by misalignment of the torch. The strength of the joint is obviously reduced. Lack of reinforcement, or insufficient build up of weld metal above the thickness of the parent metal, results in a joint likely to break in the weld.

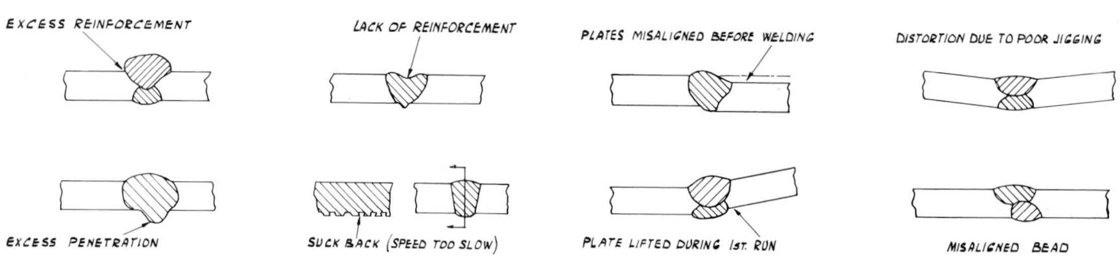

C-12 *Defects in weld shape.*

C-13 *Misalignment defects.*

The effect is similar to that obtained by machining the bead off after welding. The defect can be caused by an unsuitable welding technique or by incorrect edge preparation. Excessive reinforcement also results from choice of an unsuitable technique, while excessive penetration is due to using too high a welding current, too slow a welding speed, or a badly fitting backing bar. Both these defects, although having little effect on tensile strength, reduce the fatigue strength by increasing the notch effect at the edge of the weld. Excessive penetration can result in 'suck-back' due to shrinkage in the root pass, causing in turn a reduction in the area of the weld.

Misalignment

Poor jigging, and distortion during welding, can lead to welds being made out of line, figure C-14. There may be no significant loss of static strength in such joints, but the effect on fatigue strength can be serious.

Porosity

Porosity, common types of which are illustrated in figure C-14, has two main causes. The principal one is the presence of hydrogen, which is readily dissolved in the molten metal and which is rejected on solidification. Hydrogen may be picked up from badly prepared welding surfaces, from poor quality welding wire, or from excessive atmospheric humidity; very occasionally it is present in the parent metal and is released at the weld interface. Another cause of porosity is air which may be entrapped by molten weld metal at the base of the joint and forced to rise through the weld. The faster the welding, the more likely it is that air bubbles are entrapped. In this respect, T.I.G. welds have an advantage over M.I.G. welds due to the slower rates of cooling involved. Air entrapment may be minimised by attention to joint detail, in allowing

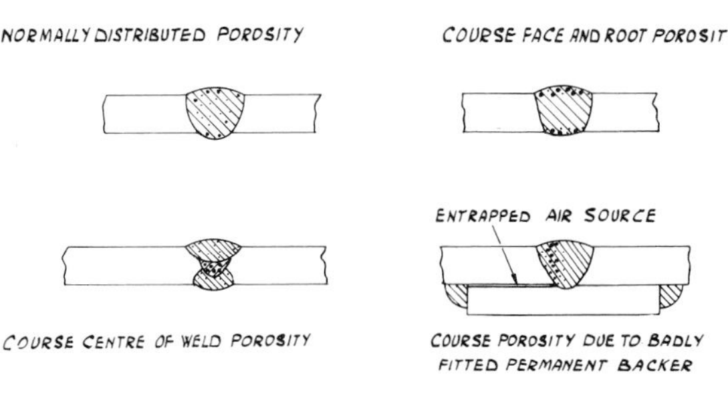

C-14 *Porosity.*

for heated air to escape by some means other than via the weld pool. The principal offenders are close-fitting joints with permanent backing bars, and square edge close-butt joints, both of which can give a line of porosity along the centre of the weld.

Linear porosity, in which the pores are concentrated in one plane parallel to the weld line, is nearly always associated with more serious defects such as lack of fusion.

Inclusions

Oxide and carbon inclusions in aluminium welds may be caused by contamination of the welding surfaces by dirt or oil. Tungsten inclusions result from overheating of the electrode, causing transfer of molten tungsten across the arc, or from contamination by contact with the weld pool. Copper inclusions can be caused by burn-back resulting in contamination from the contact tube in M.I.G. welding. Tungsten inclusions less than $\frac{1}{16}$ in. in diameter are normally considered harmless, but copper inclusions (which dissolve to some extent in aluminium), can cause cracking and constitute a serious corrosion hazard. Oxide inclusions in the form of continuous films can seriously reduce strength, but isolated patches have little effect.

Influence of defects on static strength

Among defects that have little or no influence on static properties are excess penetration and fine and medium porosity. Coarse porosity has little effect if concentrated in the top of the weld bead, but it can reduce tensile strength when concentrated at the centre of the bead. Undercutting and lack of re-inforcement can also reduce tensile strength. The efficiency of joints with the bead removed would be to the order of about 85%.

Lack of fusion can have serious effects, especially in cases where sharp open notches result.

Influence of defects on fatigue strength

The fatigue behaviour of butt welds depends principally on the shape of the re-inforcement and on whether or not the re-inforcement is removed. In the as-welded condition fatigue failure normally occurs at the edge of the bead, being due to the stress-raising effect of the change in cross section at this point. Bead shape is thus of primary importance, and imperfections inside the weld are less significant. When the bead is removed, however, flaws in the cast metal weld itself have greater significance, failure sometimes occurring through the weld.

Misalignments in butt joints increases the general stress level and can reduce the fatigue strength many times.

Inspection and testing

Inspection and testing of welded joints is necessary to obtain and maintain the required joint quality in production. The standards to which welds are inspected, will vary according to the end use of the subject weld. The methods hereby recommended are representative of good commercial practice. They may be classified under two general headings:

(1) Non-destructive testing and (2) Destructive testing.

(1) Non-destructive testing is usually carried out by three methods of examination, visual, dye penetrant, and radiography;

(a) Visual examination, particularly with the aid of a magnifying lens, will readily indicate such defects as non-uniform appearance, incomplete penetration on welds made from one side, surface cracks, undercut and overhang. Non-uniformity is not in itself a defect, but a non-uniform weld bead may well indicate the weld was not properly made, and more serious defects may be present.

(b) Dye penetrant may be used to positively locate surface cracks, surface porosity, and incomplete fusion where this extends to the surface of a weld. There are several proprietary brands of dye penetrant available, and all have their special instructions for use. The general principles are (1) clean and degrease the area, (ii) apply the dye penetrant; this finds its way into extremely small surface openings, (iii) remove the excess surface penetrant with special penetrant remover, (iv) spray the area with a fine film of developer. The surface weld defects show up in a very distinctive colour. The use of dye penetrants is not recommended by many authorities because of the difficulty of adequately cleaning the contaminated area, before a repair can be attempted. Used sparingly and with a full appreciation of the problem, they can be a quick and cheap aid.

(c) Radiography provides a permanent record of the interior condition of the weld. It is usual to x-ray butt welds only. The equipment is relatively expensive, and trained personnel are required to operate it and interpret the resulting film.

(2) Destructive testing can be classified under three main headings; fracture testing, bend testing, and tensile testing:

(a) Fracture testing is an effective and economical method of generally testing fillet and butt welds. In the case of fillet welds, one side only should be welded, and the test piece secured in a vice with the weld uppermost. The upright plate is then forced up over the weld either by adjustable spanner or hammer. A good weld should bend almost flat before breaking. Lack of fusion will be clearly shown. For testing butt welds, the nick-break is used. For this the specimen weld reinforcement and ends are notched with a saw cut, placed in a vice and the free end hammered very sharply. Examination will reveal such defects as porosity, inclusions, lack of penetration, lack of fusion, and underbead cracking (see figure C-15).

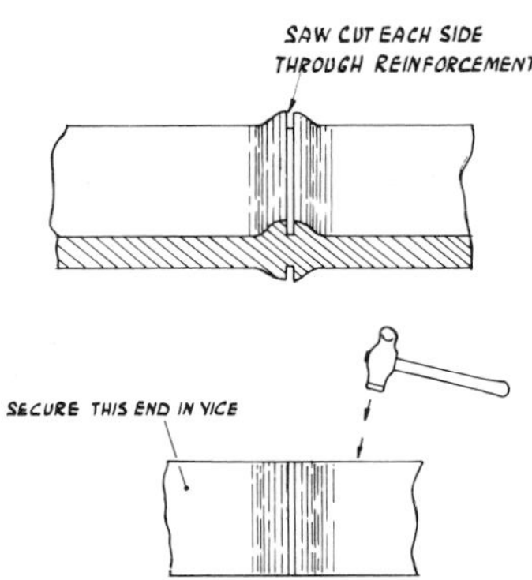

C-15 *Nick break test.*

(b) Bend testing is used on butt welds. The specimen should be cleaned of weld bead and reinforcement, and bent through 180°, around a radius of about 3T (3 × thickness of material). This test can be performed on a fly press or modified pipe bending machine.

(c) Tensile testing is carried out on a special machine to determine tensile strength, yield strength and elongation. The two sides of the welded joint are secured in the machine and the specimen pulled apart. Classification societies often call for this test to be carried out.

Safety precautions

It must surely go without saying that any complex piece of electrical equipment such as a welding machine should only be operated by trained, or under the direction of, trained personnel. Modifications to, and fault finding within the machine, must be conducted only by those qualified to do so. Many machines are fitted with elaborate safety devices, that are not necessarily essential to the working of the machine, but if the machine is operated without them, both the machine and the operator could be at risk.

Adequate ventilation, particularly in an enclosed space, should be provided in the welding area, to remove the fumes created by welding. The fumes, though relatively innocuous, can be very unpleasant when in a confined space. It is recommended that personnel working in an area where fumes are concentrated should drink an extra pint of milk each day. This is also true of where paint spraying is being carried out.

Exposure of the skin to the rays of a welding arc for even a short time, can result in a condition similar to sunburn. It is important, therefore, that the operator should protect all exposed areas of skin, particularly of the hands, head and back of the neck. Substantial dark clothing should be worn to reduce reflection. Soft leather gauntlet gloves should be worn to protect hands and arms. Helmets with recommended dark lens and lens protection should be worn. Where spatter is encountered, a leather apron should be worn in addition to other protective clothing. Wherever possible, screens should surround the welding area to protect other workers from accidental sight of the welding arc. When this does occur, it can cause great pain behind the eyes. Special eye drops are available for this condition, and if applied promptly, can eliminate or greatly reduce the suffering.

At least one qualified person should always be on the premises to render first aid, with a laid down procedure for dealing with more serious cases. Fire hazards should also be adequately provided for.

5 Fastenings

Fastenings can be divided into four main groups: (1) rivets, (2) bolts, (3) screws, (4) adhesives.

Rivets

Of all the mechanical methods of fastening, rivets are probably the most widely used. There are two general types of rivets: (a) blind, fitted from one side only, and (b) solid, fitted from one side, and points burred over on the other side.

(a) Blind rivets

These are supplied in various metals, steel, stainless steel, copper, monel and aluminium alloy, and with countersunk, or domed heads. The shank of the rivet is entered from the outside of the workpiece. A mandrel, usually steel, protrudes from the head, and is gripped in the jaws of a special tool, the jaws pull the mandrel, and in so doing, bunches up the rivet on the inside, and breaks off the mandrel at a predetermined load. The advantages are that only one operator is involved, the work can be executed from one side only, and that as the rivet is squeezed tight instead of hammered, a curved workpiece would not tend to straighten, as it does under continued hammering. Depending on the application, the rivets are supplied as 'open' or 'sealed'. In the open rivet, the mandrel is pulled right through the rivet leaving a hollow centre. These are used of course only on non-watertight joints, interior trim etc. The sealed type are supplied with a short break, or long break mandrel, and the interior is completely blanked off. In the short break, the mandrel breaks off well inside the rivet (see figure D-1); in the long break, the mandrel breaks off at the head of the rivet and is in fact exposed. The short break has the advantage of the mandrel breaking inside the rivet, leaving a smooth head, and when painted over, seals the steel mandrel inside from 'bleeding' through the paint scheme. The steel mandrel on the long break, extends just through the head and leaves a sharp edge. For appearance and safety, this has to be ground smooth.

When painted over, there is more chance of this 'bleeding' through the paint scheme. Both types of watertight rivet have the same tensile strength, but the long break has almost twice the shear strength as the short break. For all normal applications, the strength of the short break is sufficient. Only when very high shear loads are applied is the long break necessary. The most popular diameters are $\frac{1}{8}$ in. for interior, and $\frac{3}{16}$ in. for exterior applications such as superstructures etc. The length of

D-1 *'Pop' sealed type rivet setting sequence.*

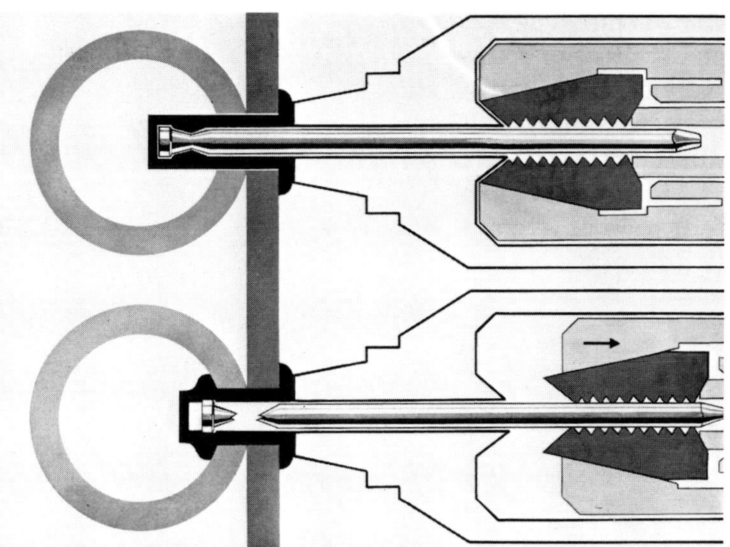

the rivet is governed by the plate thickness to be joined, sometimes called the 'grip thickness'. Tables are available from the manufacturers detailing the code by which the rivets are ordered. They also recommend hole sizes to be bored to receive the rivet.

(b) Solid rivets

As the name implies, this rivet is formed from solid bar. The manufactured head can be snap, pan, or countersunk. The points (the end that is hammered over) are usually snap or countersunk. The rivet is entered from one side of the workpiece, a 'dolly' or heavy weight is held to the head, and the point is hammered, or burred over, usually with a pneumatic reciprocating gun, fitted with a snap. The size of snap, is determined by the diameter of the rivet. The hammering over can be done by hand in the smaller diameters, but is not recommended for the larger rivets, because of the work hardening effect of the hammering (i.e., becoming brittle when worked). A relatively few heavy blows applied quickly tend to provide a tighter joint. A good general formula for the rivet length $L = 1.10 \times$ grip thickness $+ 1.15 \times$ diameter of rivet. Solid rivets can be obtained in diamters from $\frac{1}{16}$ in. to $\frac{3}{8}$ in. in increments of $\frac{1}{32}$ in.

The choice of blind or solid rivets will depend chiefly on cost, appearance, availability, and whether both sides of the workpiece are accessible. Some operators consider there is more control over the amount the solid rivet can be drawn up. The solid rivet is cheaper, but the operation is very much noisier.

The material for the rivet should be as similar as available to the parent metal. If the parent metal is N.S. 8 aluminium alloy, normally the closest rivet material is N.E. 6 and this is quite compatible.

Where a watertight joint is required, the faying or mating surfaces, and the rivet shank, should be wet assembled with a suitable elastomer. Berger Chemicals produce an excellent one known as P.R.C. Rubber Calk 150, and is a two-part Polysulphide Rubber. Both mating surfaces should be degreased and lightly coated immediately prior to joining. The mixture usually has a limited life when mixed, so only the minimum quantity should be mixed at a time.

The simplest form of riveted joint is the lap joint, which may have one, two, three or four rows of rivets.

Butt straps are also used, with either single or double rows of rivets (see figure D-2).

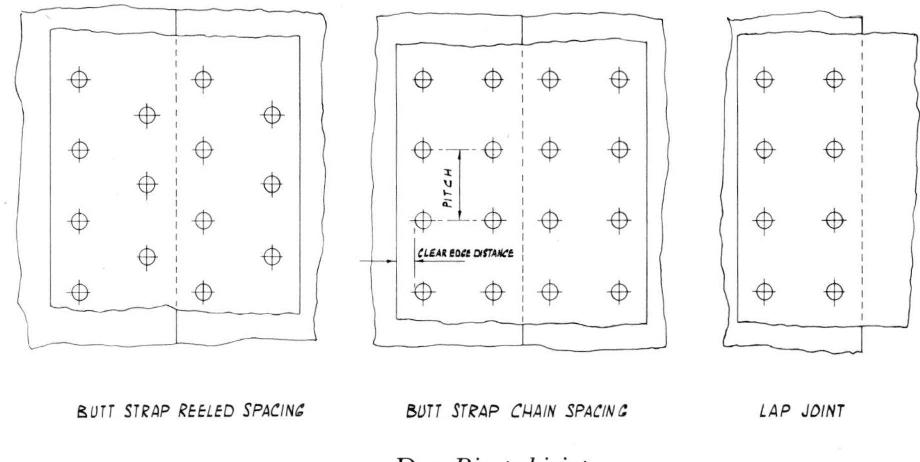

D-2 *Riveted joints.*

When building to classification society rules, their rule book gives the diameter, pitch, spacing between rows, and distance of rivets from the plate edge, for each piece of structure. For Admiralty work, pitch is normally given as:

Maximum: $4\frac{1}{2}$ diameters in oiltight work
5 diameters in watertight work
8 diameters otherwise

Clear distance from edge of plate, one diameter + $\frac{1}{8}$ in.

Bolts

Depending on location and strength requirements, these will normally be galvanised mild steel or stainless steel.

Above the water line, or for internal structure, where a strength requirement not exceeding about 28 tons per square in. U.T.S. is sufficient, galvanised mild steel would be suitable,

Zinc plating will not protect mild steel against seawater indefinitely. Painting with etch primer plus a full paint scheme is recommended.

Below the water line, or where the strength factor demands are greater, stainless steel should be used. Where the risk of corrosion is greatest—i.e., immersed in salt water, 18/8 austenitic stainless steel cadmium plated, would considerably reduce galvanic corrosion.

All bimetal joints and all joints of wood to metal should be met assembled with a suitable jointing compound.

Nuts should, wherever possible, be of a similar material to the bolts they secure. Cadmium plated steel nuts, on cadmium plated stainless steel bolts, though not ideal, is sometimes an acceptable compromise. Various new types of locknuts are now available; among the more usual are—the 'slipnot', a self-locking nut, embodying a collet-like frictional metallic grip; the 'slitnot', this has an axially stretched neck; the 'nylock', with a nylon insert, the nylon initially has a plain bore, but when the nut is screwed tight, a thread is cut into the nylon and grips very tightly around the bolt. These newer types of locknuts are tending to supersede the older second locknut, spring washers, and castle nuts with split pins. It is sometimes very useful to attach a temporary or permanent thread to the workpiece. This can, of course, be done by tapping a thread if the parent metal is thick enough. Putting a thread into aluminium has limitations though, because of the softness of aluminium and its alloys. The danger exists of stripping the thread, so more threads than normal are required. It is quite usual for tapped aluminium bosses to be welded to aluminium tanks, to receive valves etc. A word of warning here; an aluminium shank must never be screwed into an aluminium tapped hole. Before a couple of threads had been entered, the whole thing would grind together, and be very difficult to part. Where it is necessary to provide a deep tapped hole in thin sheet metal, 'hank' rivet bushes are often used. These are produced by several manufacturers and in various threads and sizes. Where needs are for water-tightness, a blank end can be supplied. The 'hank' bush is essentially a nut, with a collar, that is entered into a hole in the workpiece and riveted over (see figure D-3 p. 54).

Anchor nuts are also extensively used; these consist of a captive nut retained in a cage, this is in turn riveted to the workpiece. The nuts can be either fixed or floating to provide greater flexibility in lining up. There are many other types of captive nut for specialist applications.

Another very useful method of attaching a thread is with a 'Heli-Coil'. This is a stainless steel screw thread insert. A hole is drilled in the workpiece and is then tapped with special 'Heli-Coil' tap. The stainless steel insert is then wound into the tapped hole with a special inserting tool. Where the thickness of metal is sufficient, and the bolt needs to be tightened hard, these inserts are very popular. They are quick to install, not over expensive, and can be worked from one side only. Once in position, they will not work loose, but can be extracted with a special tool.

D-3 *Hank bush.*

D-4 *'Dzus' Fastener.*

Another method of retaining a panel in position is with a 'Dzus' fastener. This consists of a receptacle riveted to the parent metal, and a bolt held captive in the panel. The bolt is screwed into the receptacle with a special coarse quick action thread, and is retained in the panel with a grommet (see figure D-4).

Screws

Self tapping screws are sometimes used in thin panels, but the thread in the aluminium tends to strip after a few tightenings.

Adhesives

Where adhesive bonding is used for attaching insulation and trim on boats, the rubber-base compounds are often used. Resin-type coatings are also suitable where curing takes place at room temperature and simple fixing jigs can be employed.

For making structural joints between aluminium surfaces, several high strength adhesives are availabe. Some of these require curing by tightly controlled applications of heat and mating pressures. This calls for special ovens and complex fixing jigs. Only considerable volume throughput would justify the initial capital investment.

Adhesives are not widely used in low production aluminium boatbuilding. This may be due to traditional conservatism, or lack of knowledge. There is need for experimentation in choice of adhesive, design of joint, and technique of application. It is highly possible that adhesives will figure more prominently in the joining of aluminium in the future.

6 Lines and Laying Off

It is not the intention here to describe in great detail the manner in which a set of lines is assembled by the designer, and laid off by the loftsman. These basic principles appear in so many publications that a repetition is unwarranted. For the uninitiated, however, a very brief outline is set out.

Lines plans are the traditional graphic method by which a designer can indicate to the builder in three dimensional form, the shape the vessel shall take. Three views are necessary, profile or sheer, half breadth or plan view, and body plan or half sections. It is necessary to draw full size all views, for it is only when the lines passing through the same points in each view, all fair, can we be certain that when the plating is fitted, the individual plates will all present a continuous and pleasing curve. A table of offsets is provided to enable the basic lines to be drawn. These offsets, i.e., dimensions measured from particular datum lines, are taken about station lines. These station lines are positioned solely for the convenience of the designer, and the reason we have to duplicate full size what he has provided us with to a small scale, is simply to prove his accuracy.

Sometimes, when working to the dimensions given, or offsets, the lines will not fair in all three views. It is the loftsman's job to ensure that all the views do fair, and where necessary, correct the offsets. A typical lines plan is shown in figure E-1 p. 56.

With the buttock lines faired in the profile and the waterlines faired in the half breadth, verticals are raised at all bulkhead and frame stations. From these two views, a new body plan can be drawn indicating half sections at all these new station positions. We can now produce templates to indicate the outline of all frames and bulkheads. Only half the section need be produced, because we can turn the template over and work about the centreline.

Longitudinal or fore and aft members such as stem and keel, engine beds, stringers, spray rails, chines, gunwales etc., can now be drawn in and templates made as necessary.

Templates are best produced from solid material such as sheets of ply or hardboard. If produced from framed material such as slats of wood around the perimeter, with struts holding them together, there is a great danger of distortion. The templates are used to mark the outline of the section onto the aluminium sheets. The sheets or extrusions are then tacked together and checked with the templates. Where distortion has occurred, it must corrected, and then finally welded.

When very large sheets are used for the skin, or where a lot of shape is encountered,

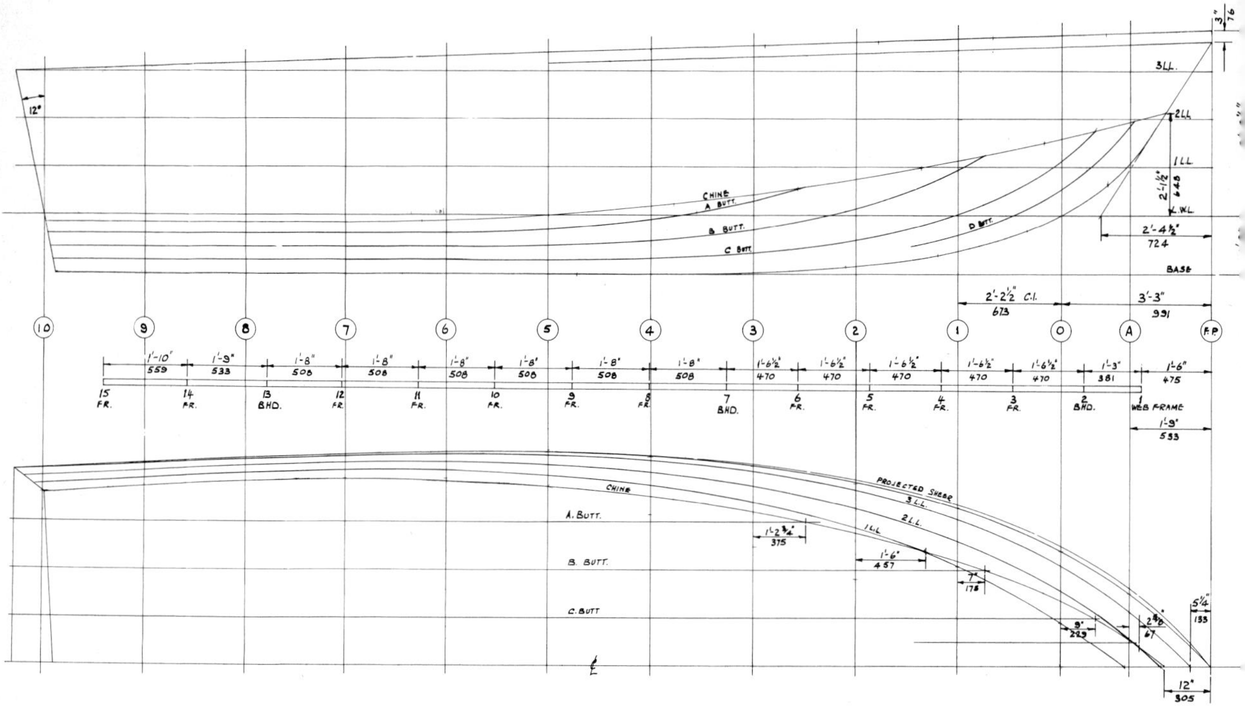

TABLE OF OFFSETS

NUMBER OF STATIONS		A	0	1	2	3	4	5	6	7	8	9	10	
HEIGHTS ABOVE BASE	PROJECTED SHEER			STRAIGHT LINE F.P. TO STN. 10									4-3-2	INCHES
													1301	m.m.
	BUTTOCK C	3-1-2	2-4-4	1-3-2	0-8-4	0-5-3	0-4-0	0-3-4	STRAIGHT LINE				0-3-4	INCHES
		946	724	387	216	137	102	89						m.m.
	BUTTOCK B	—	—	2-2-2	1-4-4	0-11-2	0-8-4	0-7-1	0-6-7	STRAIGHT LINE			0-6-7	INCHES
		—	—	667	419	286	216	181	165				165	m.m.
	BUTTOCK A	—	—	—	—	1-6-4	1-1-6	0-11-2	0-10-3	STRAIGHT LINE			0-10-3	INCHES
		—	—	—	—	470	349	286	264				264	m.m.
	CHINE	3-2-2	2-10-0	2-4-4	1-11-7	1-8-0	1-5-1	1-3-0	1-1-4	1-1-0	STRAIGHT LINE		1-1-0	INCHES
		972	864	724	606	508	435	381	343	330			330	m.m.
	KEEL	2-4-0	1-3-0	0-5-7	0-2-0	0-0-3	—	—	—	—	—	—	—	INCHES
		711	381	149	51	10	—	—	—	—	—	—	—	m.m.
HALF BREADTHS	PROJECTED SHEER	1-7-4	2-6-0	3-4-4	3-10-6	4-2-5	4-4-5	4-5-6	4-5-5	4-4-7	4-4-7	4-2-6	4-1-2	INCHES
		495	762	1029	1177	1286	1337	1365	1362	1343	1321	1289	1251	m.m.
	3 L.L.	1-1-6	2-1-1	3-0-6	3-8-1	4-0-6	4-3-4	4-4-7	4-5-0	4-4-3	4-3-5	4-2-3	4-1-1	INCHES
		349	638	933	1121	1238	1308	1343	1346	1330	1311	1280	1248	m.m.
	2 L.L.	0-7-0	1-6-7	2-7-2	3-3-4	3-9-1	4-0-3	4-2-3	4-3-1	4-2-7	4-2-0	4-0-6	3-11-3	INCHES
		178	479	784	1003	1146	1229	1280	1299	1292	1270	1238	1203	m.m.
	1 L.L.	—			2-10-5	3-5-0	3-9-2	3-11-5	4-1-0	4-1-0	4-0-1	3-10-7	3-9-3	INCHES
		—			879	1041	1149	1210	1245	1245	1222	1181	1153	m.m.
	CHINE	0-6-5	1-4-3	2-2-2	2-9-3	3-2-5	3-6-4	3-9-0	3-10-2	3-10-6	3-10-1	3-8-6	3-7-0	INCHES
		168	416	667	848	981	1080	1143	1175	1187	1172	1137	1092	m.m.

DIMENSIONS IN FEET INCHES & EIGHTHS OF AN INCH & MILLIMETRS TO INSIDE OF SKIN

PRINCIPAL DIMENSIONS

LENGTH OVERALL ...... 26'-0"
MOULDED BEAM MAX. ...... 8'-11½"
MOULDED CHINE BEAM MAX. ...... 7'-9½"
MOULDED DEPTH .... 4'-7¾"

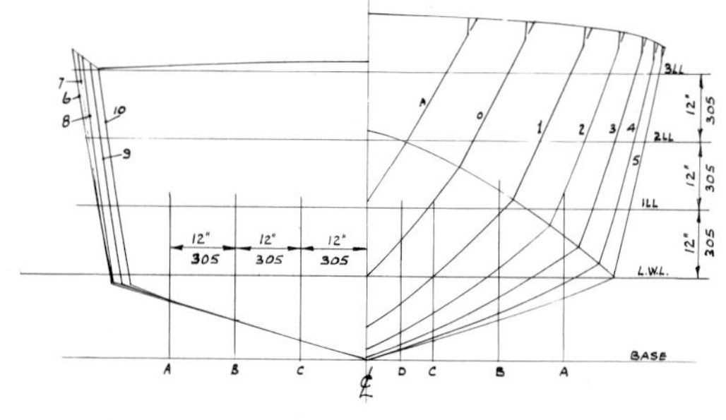

E-1 *Typical Lines plan.*

it is sometimes necessary, or at least very convenient, to predetermine the final shape of the hull plating. One method by which this is achieved is by triangulation. This enables us to develop a curved surface onto a flat plane. On a chine boat this is often only considered necessary in the fore part of the bottom, although of course it can be

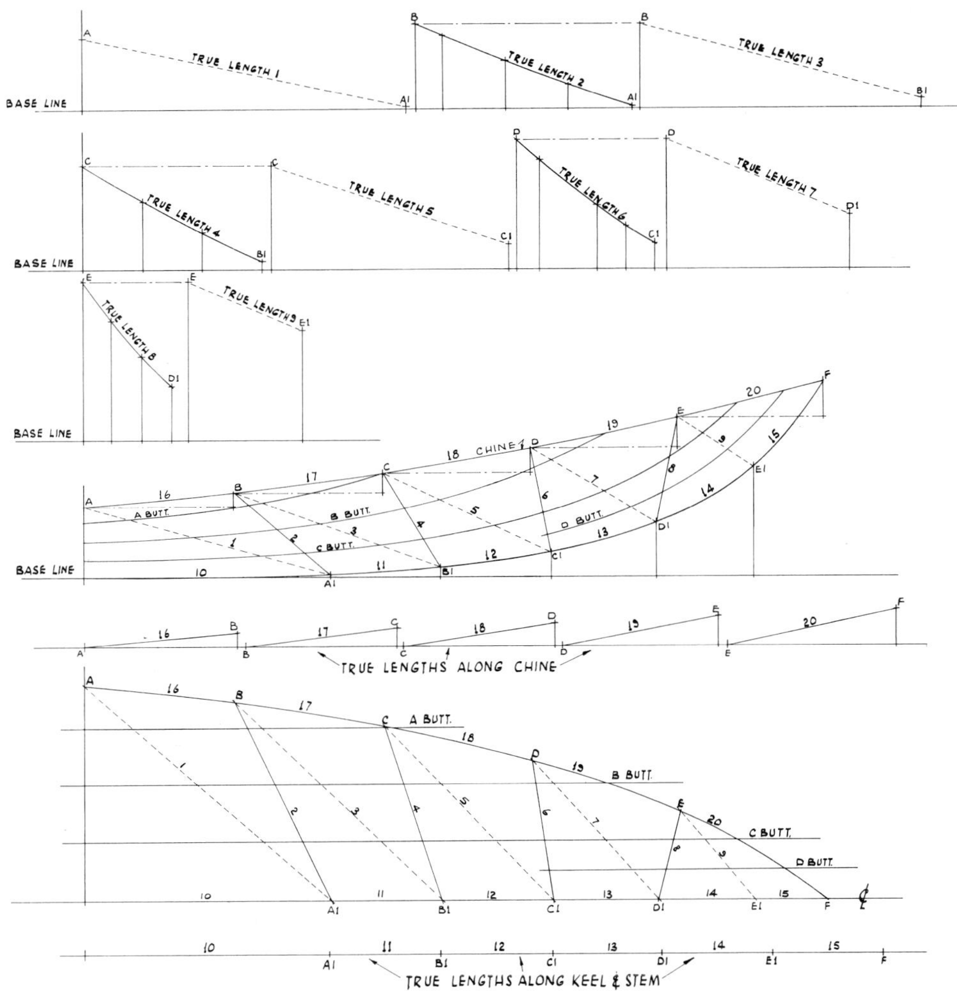

E-2 *Development of true lengths for triangulation.*

used on any part of the hull. The surface is divided up into a number of adjoining triangles as in fig. A-3 p. 18. By drawing diagonal lines from chine to keel, the surface is triangulated for development (see figure E-2). To lay out or develop the hull surface, the true lengths of all sides of all triangles must be determined. This is accomplished by the use of right triangles. The length of one side of these triangles as they appear in the plan is used for the base, and their differences in elevation, as they appear in the profile, is used for the vertical height. By laying out these two lines at right angles to each other, the length of the hypotenuse, which is the true length, is determined. The true lengths are now used as radii of arcs which are intersected to form the final flat expansion. The diagonals which are curved are determined from the buttock

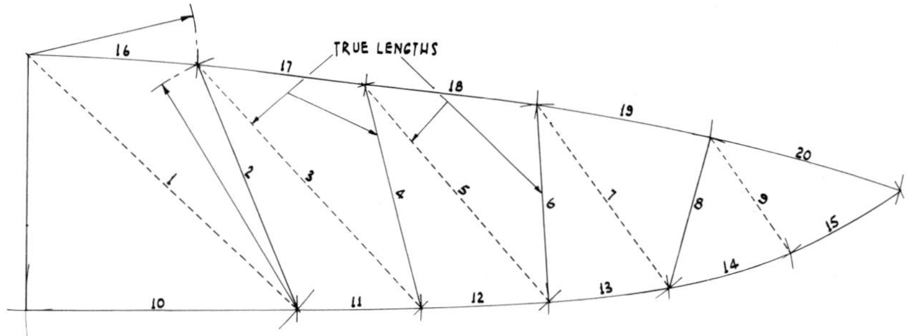

E-3 *Expansion of forward bottom plate by triangulation.*

intersections much in the same way as the frames. Their true lengths are determined by girthing the curve. By building up the triangles in a continuous line, the final shape of the sheet is determined (see figure E-3).

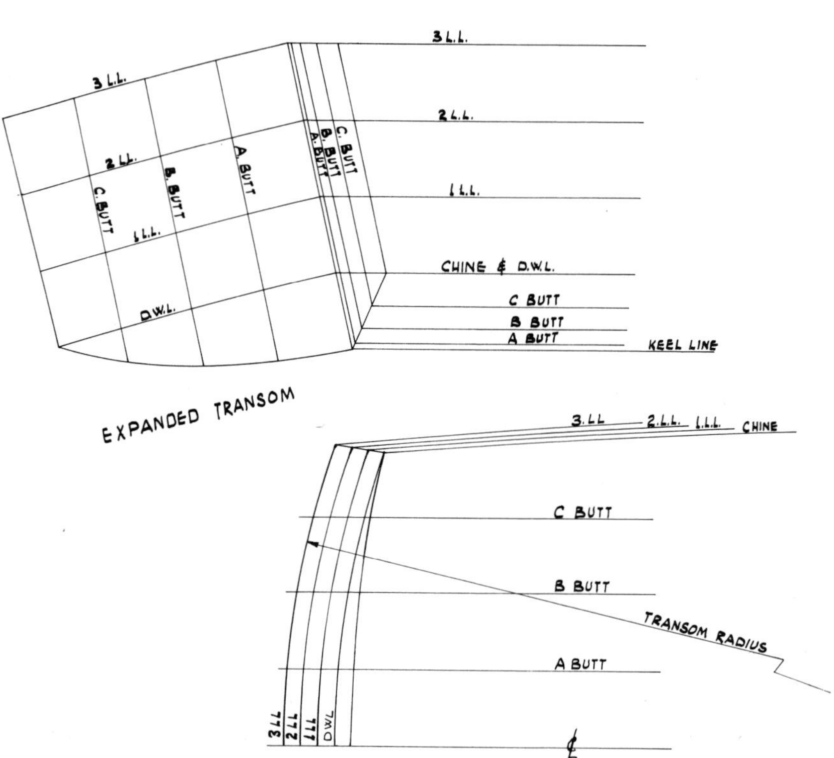

E-4 *Development of expanded transom.*

Where a curved transom is required, it is necessary to produce an expanded view—i.e., when the transom is unwrapped, so that it can be cut out of flat plates, and when shaped, the periphery will line up with the extension of the plating. There are several ways of developing or producing an expanded view of the transom. A fairly straightforward way is illustrated in figure E-4. This indicates the profile and plan view of the aft section of a vessel with a rounded transom.

The radius is shown in the plan view with the centre line of the arc struck from the centreline of the boat. Also shown in both views are three buttock lines 'A', 'B' and 'C', and three waterlines 1, 2 and 3. To obtain the expanded view of the transom, all that is necessary is to unwrap the transom by flattening it out; at the same time flatten out the waterlines and buttocks, and by measuring these round the shaped transom with a batten, straighten out the batten, and by transferring and projecting these new marks on to our expanded view and obtaining a series of spots on our newly drawn waterlines and buttocks, these indicate the extremities of the expanded transom. By joining these spots with a fair line the periphery of the transom is completed.

To take this a step at a time. On the profile, continue the waterlines normal to the rake or slope of the transom. Lay a batten around the curve of the transom and on it mark the position of the buttock lines. Straighten out the batten, and mark in these expanded buttock lines. We now have a grid of expanded buttocks and waterlines laying normal to the slope of the transom. By projecting the termination of the buttock lines in the profile to obtain the heights, and measuring round the curved waterlines in the plan view to obtain the half breadths, then straightening out the batten and transferring these spots on the relative waterlines in the expanded view, and as already indicated, by joining these spots with a fair line, we have the expanded view of the transom.

Where there is a lot of shape in the hull, as for some round bilge boats, it may be necessary to draw in extra buttocks or waterlines, to obtain extra spots to enable a more accurate curve to be drawn.

Laying off demands a high degree of accuracy in measuring and marking. Any inaccuracies must be resolved in the three views. If they are not, problems will inevitably arise when fairing in the hull.

The scrieve board—i.e., the area where the lines are laid down, must be flat and kept free of all traffic. A set of lines accurately and well set out, if preserved, can be of great value throughout the entire build time of the vessel. It is often very time saving to have the opportunity to refer back to the full size lines for a multitude of dimensional requirements, particularly in connection with sterngear.

7 Jigs

The amount of jig making will to some extent depend on the number of craft to be built to the same design, or the number of precisely similar parts to a craft. Jigs can be broadly divided into two classes: the essential jigs that have to be produced in order to build the craft, and convenience jigs that are produced in order to save time where quantity production is involved.

The building jig is the largest and most important one, and ranges from simple building blocks to a master assembly-welding fixture, which is supported at each end by trunnion swivel mountings that can be rotated to bring any desired portion of the hull to the top. One company in the U.S.A. produces a 14 ft. runabout, on such a jig where gunwales, stem, keel and chine extrusions are clamped in position, after which the hull plating is fitted and clamped in position. A series of pneumatic holding clamps, actuated from a control console, pulls the sheets and extrusions together to produce the proper welding gap. Circuit lights indicate when each hull section is properly positioned. An automatically guided welding gun runs on a roller track. The welding head is suspended and can be raised or lowered automatically, as well as moved longitudinally during welding.

A set of timing circuits, all connected to the control console, makes the welding operation substantially automatic. Only two persons, the console operator and a man to place the aluminium sheets and extrusions on the frame, are required. Circulating water is run to the welding gun and also to the chill bars which are permanent elements of the welding fixture, and are located to bear against the hull plates where welding heat input is concentrated. Seam welding with this equipment proceeds at the rate of about four feet per minute.

There are many variations from the simplest to the sophisticated jig described above. The determining factor is; over how many craft can the cost of the jig be amortized. There can be no doubt that, given the correct set up, the labour cost of producing an aluminium hull, can be as cheap or cheaper than, any other form of construction.

A typical simple building jig is illustrated in figure F-1. This is for a 75-ft. chine boat. Fig. F-2 p. 62 shows the jig constructed and the forward bulkheads being set up. The jig consists essentially of two steel channel sections following very broadly the outline of the sheer in plan form, with a similar channel on the centre line. Bolted to these three channels, are steel angles, with the upright outside face directly positioned on each bulkhead and frame station. The whole jig is levelled by means of the jacking

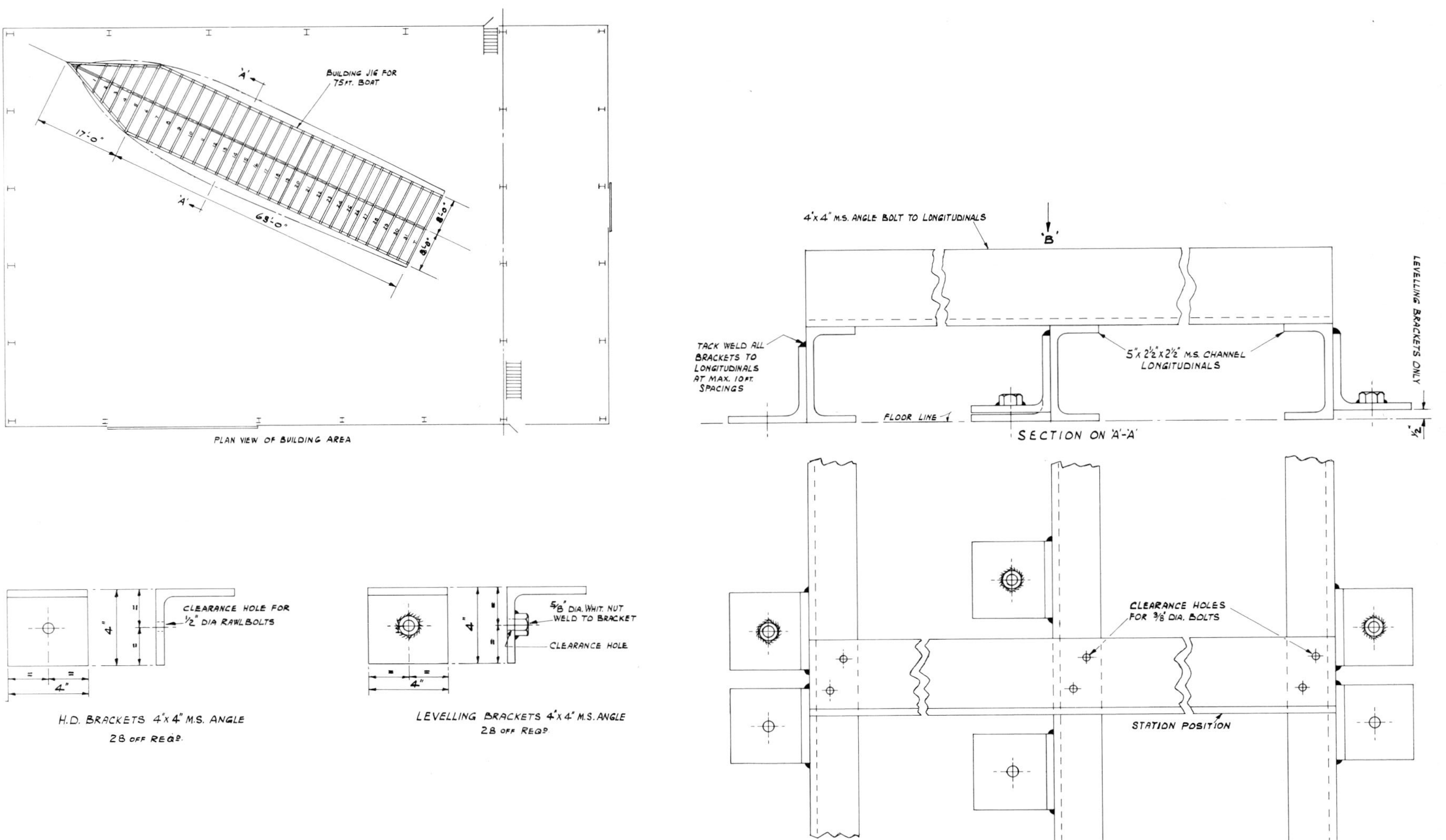

F-1 *Building jig for 75 foot boat.*

F-2 *Jig with bulkheads set up.*

F-3 *Wooden former for curved transom.*

screws, and bolted to the concrete floor, using distance pieces under the securing lugs as necessary. We now have a datum face and centre line to work to. The bulkheads and frames are set up on light gauge steel angles and braced together.

When the hull has been completed and is ready for turning over, the jig is left in position, and hull and jig are turned as one unit. The jig gives rigidity to the hull and prevents any possibility of distortion during the turning operation.

Where a curved transom is required, a wooden former such as that illustrated in figure F-3 is simple to construct. The face of the wooden former should be concave, so that after forming by the rollers, the transom plates are laid and secured temporarily to the wooden framing. The aluminium stiffeners are then shaped and positioned, and welding completed.

Where unit construction is used—i.e., whole parts are sub-assembled, very precise and substantial jigs are necessary, so that mating parts will match. This type of construction, though more expensive on jigging, does enable more operators to be employed at one time and can considerably reduce the overall building time, and occupancy, of the building berth.

The building jigs so far described, have been on the assumption of building upside down. The advantages so outweight the disadvantages, provided there is room and equipment to execute the turnover, that it is difficult to conceive building upright from choice. Let us consider some of the advantages. All the frame work and strutting can be contained within the perimeters of the hull. Once the hull plates are lifted into approximate position gravity holds them there. Welding is to a very large extent all downhand, and this alone would make it worthwhile. Temporary strutting of plates in position is eliminated. Plates can be finally positioned with greater accuracy. More plates can be welded together off the job because of the easier assembly. It is considerably easier to position and true up the bulkheads and frames. The stem head can be secured to a substantial base. Because the jig is heavy and rigid there is far less

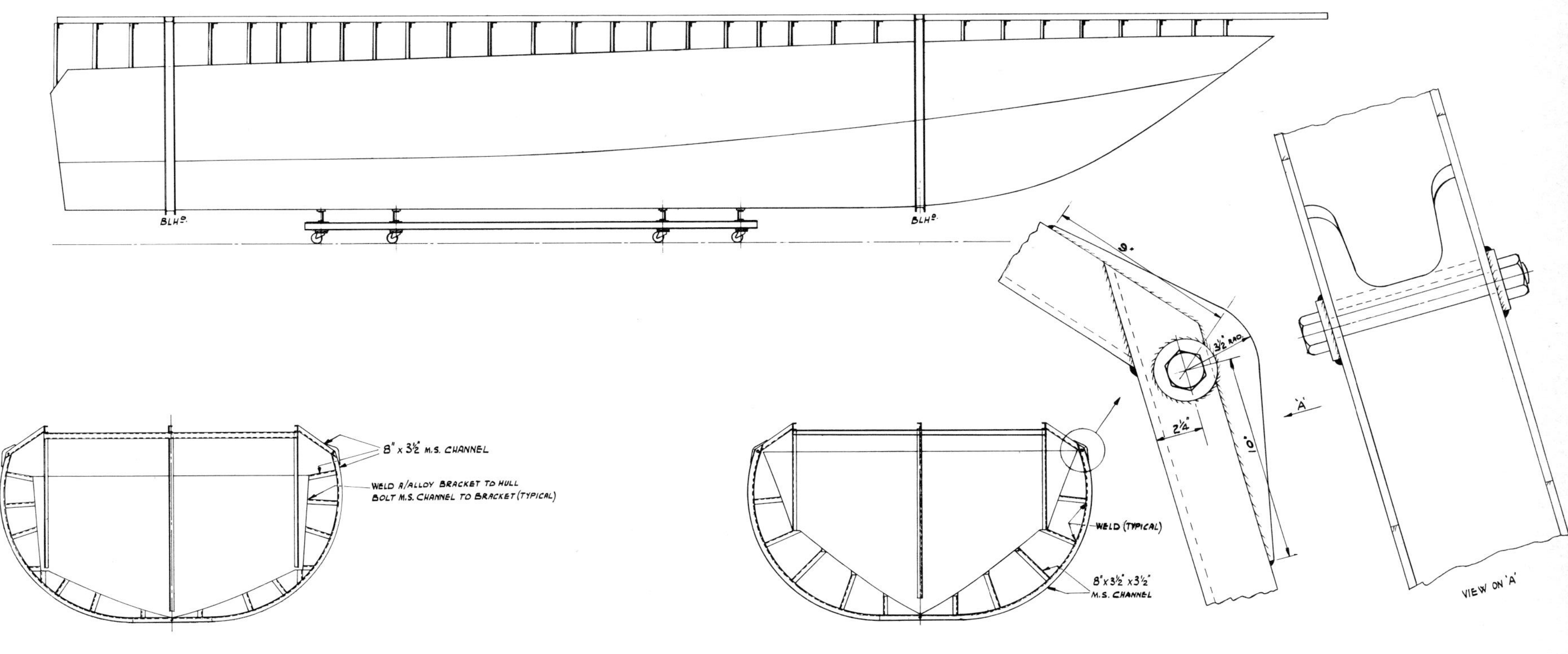

F-4 *Roll over hoops for 75 ft boat.*

F-5 *Turning over 75 ft hull.*

possibility of serious welding distortion. From the safety angle, there is less chance of cramps becoming loosened and plates falling.

The big disadvantage is that the vessel has to be turned. This can be accomplished by one of two methods: turning in situ, by means of a revolving jig, or rolling over on hoops secured to the hull after completion.

The revolving jig has the advantage of requiring less turning space, but is probably restricted to smaller vessels up to about 50 ft. in length. Otherwise, very substantial and expensive rollers would have to be used.

Roll over hoops as illustrated in fig. F-4 p. 63 could be used on almost any size vessel. They consist of fairly heavy channel section shaped in a curve, not necessarily a segment of a circle, or they could even be a series of flats. The completed hoop is secured to the hull and the building jig for rigidity and one or preferably two cranes or lifting chain tackles if a small craft, secured to the base of each hoop on one side and lifts. When lifted to beyond top dead centre, the whole unit completes the journey to upright position by its own weight. Figures F-5 illustrate the operation.

8 Fabrication and Setting Up

The design will, to a very large extent, determine the fabrication and setting up of our vessel. Such things as; what items are intercostal, which continuous, whether bulkheads are watertight, are there integral tanks, is the design based on longitudinal or transverse framing, or a combination of both. Is the vessel to be built by unit construction, what lifting gear is available, will it be built upside down; we must even consider at this stage how it will be launched.

The Shipyard Manager must, before the job is started, plan each sequence of operations, starting at launching, and provide a logical regression of events. This may not be so necessary with smaller boats, say under 40 ft. but when the overall length is above 60 ft. and launching weight above 30 tons, a general plan is essential. The details can be the subject of discussion as the job progresses. But it would be very unfortunate to, say, build the vessel upside down, and then find it cannot be turned over, for lack of gear or space. In setting up it is not enough to be planning the next step, but two or three steps ahead. In this way, many pitfalls can be avoided.

The laying off, and making of templates, has been described in a previous chapter. Using the bulkhead templates, mark off the outline with a scriber on to the appropriate plates, cut out and weld. As the welding proceeds, check for distortion and correct. If the design calls for stiffeners running in one direction only, say vertical, it may be necessary to weld on temporary stiffeners horizontally, to counteract the transverse distortion that would otherwise occur. In welding large flat areas such as full bulkheads, it is very easy to build in distortion, unless precautions are taken. The largest plates possible should be used and sequences adopted, as described in the chapter on welding, to minimise distortion. Any large holes or openings for doorways should be cut out after all the welding has been completed. The same procedure should be used for the engine beds, if, as is usual, they form part of the main structure.

Before erection of any of the bulkheads, datum lines must be transferred from the templates on to the bulkheads with lightly scribed lines. These will normally consist of the centre line, datum waterline, and a level line near the sheer line.

Assuming the boat is to be built upside down, consideration must be given as to whether the deck should be constructed, and used as a jig for setting up the bulkheads and frames, or whether a separate jig should be used. It is probably more straightforward, though a little more expensive on materials, to build on a separate jig. Transverses will have been secured to the jig in way of all frame and bulkhead stations, a centreline will be prominently marked on all transverses, and the jig will be set up level longitudinally and transversely. A spirit level alone is not sufficiently accurate over long distances. A water level, or preferably surveyors level, should be used. If we are to use the jig (and it is sensible to do so) as our datum for setting up the framing, it is essential that this be level all ways. Before setting up can commence, a common distance must be decided upon from the level line on the framing to a common level on the jig. This should be determined by allowing a minimum of about 18 in. gap between the lowest part of the sheer and the jig, so that when the plating is in position, sufficient room is left for a man to crawl through.

The main bulkheads and transom may now be erected on the appropriate stations, making sure that the centre line and level line are in accord with the jig. A plumb bob will be used to position the centre line, and a water level the level lines. Temporary steel angles through bolted, should connect the bulkheads to the jig, and be securely stayed with struts. If, as is often the case, the minor frames are intercostal to the keel and engine beds, the keel and engine beds should now be erected and welded in position. We now have a backbone, and terminal points to which we can attach the frames, (see figure G-1). Level lines should be scribed to all frames prior to erection. There will be many occasions later when it is necessary to obtain a positioning datum within the hull, and this is the most accurate way to obtain it. With all the bulkheads, transom, engine beds, and frames in position, stringers, chines, and gunwales, should be prepared. When the stringers are slotted into the frames, and the laying off is to a very high standard, the stringer slots could be cut into the frames prior to erection. Should there be a doubt of the precise accuracy, the stringer slots should be faired in after frame erection, and cut out. It may take a little more time to cut in the slots, but it would save time if the slots have to be re-positioned and the redundant holes plugged. Now is the time, whilst there is accessibility, to fit the interior bracketry that is normally called for on the design. Wherever possible, welding in way of integral tanks should be carried out, before the restrictions of plating. The framework must

G-1 *Early erection of framing.*

now be faired prior to plating. This is done with a dreadnought file, or grinder. It must be carefully carried out with constant checking with fairing batten, athwartships and longitudinally. It is very easy to fair the frames, and find there is a hollow in the stringers at that point, or vice-versa. It is this operation that very largely determines the shape of the hull. Any unfairness in the structure will be transferred to the plating and will be very difficult to eradicate.

Waterways should be cut into structure on the bottom, that will enable the bilge water to drain to the strum boxes.

The shell expansion drawing will indicate where the plating butts pass through stringers and frames. Notches should be cut out to enable the welding to be continuous (see figure G-2).

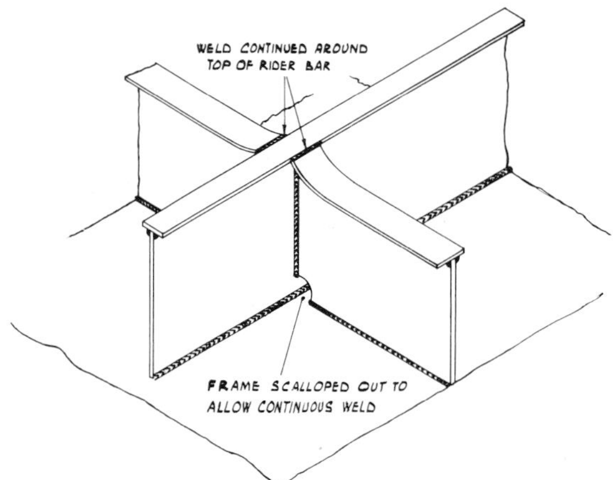

G-2 *Welding continuity.*

During the whole period of frame erection a constant watch should be kept on the centreline of the keel. This must be maintained in a straight line, otherwise a steering bias could be built in. Welding must progress evenly from side to side, aiming constantly at equalisation or cancellation of welding stresses. This also applies to engine beds, which should be kept as straight as possible.

If shaft tunnels are called for, these also should be fitted and welded in position.

If the vessel is to be built right side up, the procedure is generally similar, except that the keel and stem are laid down first, and the bulkheads erected on them. Two verticals well braced and slightly further apart than the length of the boat, and slightly higher than the sheer, with a taut wire stretched between them, provides a datum from which a plumb bob can be suspended, to centre the keel and stem, and align the centreline of the bulkheads.

The keel will be set up either on keel blocks, a little taller than the launching trolley which will enable it to be positioned after plating is completed, or on the launching

G-3 *Welding must progress evenly from side to side.*

trolley itself. Custom of the yard and availability of lifting gear will almost predetermine the choice. The building base should preferably be set up level longitudinally to the waterlines, as this will allow plain spirit levels to be used during construction, and it can also be used to obtain a vertical datum from a water line. If this is not possible, a declination piece will have to be added to the base of the spirit level, at the same incline as the waterlines. This can be a great nuisance and should be avoided if possible. With the keel and stem well secured in position with temporary struts, a main bulkhead as near midships as possible should be erected. This will be our master bulkhead, and great care should be exercised to ensure it is upright, and set at 90° to the centreline of the keel. The sheer and chine, or bilge should be horned in to the centreline of the stem—e.g., the opposite point on the bulkhead should measure the same amount to the stem. When this master bulkhead is correctly and securely positioned, the other bulkheads, moving forward and aft, can be positioned in relation to it. Engine beds, frames and stringers will follow as previously described.

9 Hull Plating

It will already have been agreed between the designer and builder, the general overall size of the hull plates, and the shell expansion drawing will have been issued indicating the position of all the butts. Commensurate with the lifting gear available, and the curvature of the hull, the largest sheets available should be used. This will obviously reduce the amount of welding, so saving time, and will usually result in a fairer hull, For reasons of availability it is sometimes necessary to accept smaller sheet sizes. When this is so, as much welding should be done off the job as is practicable. This will enable backing bars to be used, with a single pass. Usually a neater weld, requiring less cleaning, and a stronger weld with less faults.

Where a high standard of lofting is available, laying off, or marking the perimeter of the plates, is no problem, as this can be done direct from the loft floor or scrieve board. Where there is a doubt, it will be necessary either to lift the plates in position, or make templates, to suit the marks on the framing that have been transferred from the shell expansion drawing. The cheapest quality of hardboard is well suited for this, and gives a fair indication of how the aluminium sheet will lie in position, and if much shaping will be required.

Whether to commence plating from the sheer or keel, is largely a personal preference. If the vessel is built upside down it may well be easier to start from the keel down and where built right way up to work from the sheer down. This will provide for a longer period, easier access to the inside of the hull. An advantage in building upside down is that when plating, especially the bottom on a chine boat, the plates will rest in position without the necessity for external supports. All that is needed are a few cramps around the perimeter. For plates of up to about 8 mm. where the curvature is small and regular, cramps are normally all that is necessary to pull the plate to the framing. It is better to pull the plates down under a little pressure as this will ensure the plates are touching down on the centre, and it gives a fairer line to the finished hull. For plates thicker than this, and where there are complex curves, it will be necessary to shape the plates. The really thick plates, in excess of 12 mm., are normally only required in way of propeller brackets, and these being right at the aft end require rolling only. Where double curvature occurs, it may be necessary to use the wheeling machine to provide 'belly' in the centre of the plate, and if the periphery needs a little shrinking this can quite simply be done on the 'Eckold' shaper. Putting shape into an aluminium plate, provided the right gear, and a little knowhow is available, should present no great problem. It is not necessary or desirable to completely shape the contour of the hull, the final pulling down to shape, should be left to the cramps.

Where there is plating of different thicknesses, it is easier to place the thicker plates in position first, especially if, as is usual, the extra thickness has to be removed from the framing to allow a flush exterior. At the initial stage, all the plates should be tacked into position first, to minimise distortion, and also you may have a need to remove one if, for instance, it is not laying fair. Both sides of the hull should be worked simultaneously, or alternately, for equalisation of welding stresses.

For plate butts that have to be welded on the hull, one of three methods can be used.
(1) A permanent backing bar can either be built into the hull, or a part of structure could be used as such. The backer would have to be welded to the skin, but there is no simple way of checking the degree of penetration.
(2) A M.I.G. root pass is laid on the inside of the skin, back chipped, and final pass or passes laid on the outside.
(3) A T.I.G. root pass is laid from the outside of the skin, back chipped, and final pass or passes laid on the outside. If T.I.G. is available, it would probably make a neater job and require less cleaning up.

There are many and various small aids, most of them fabricated from scrap, the operator will make for himself, to assist in placing and precisely positioning the plates. Some of these are shown in figure H-1. These usually incorporate some kind of wedge that will force the butts together longitudinally and vertically, whilst they are being tacked. They can then be dispensed with when full welding takes place. If the gap

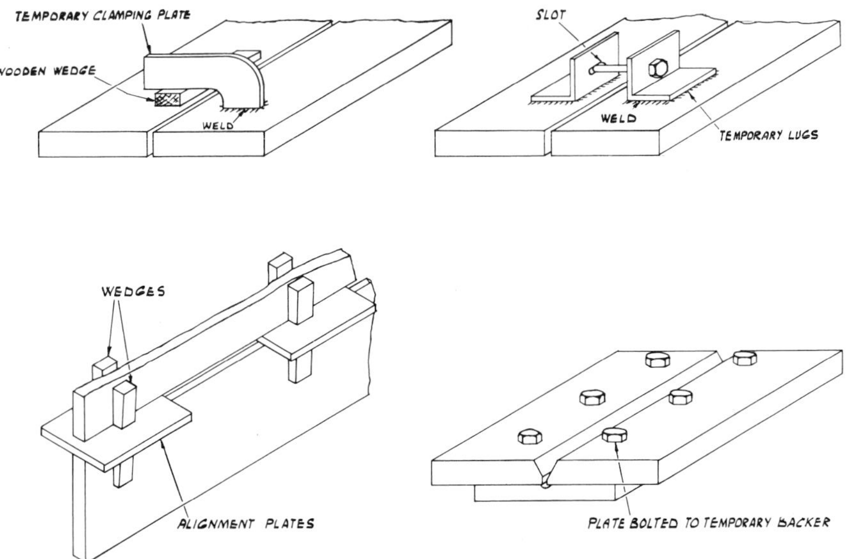

H-1 *Simple plate welding jigs.*

between the butts permits, small bolts with washer plates and nuts could be inserted and screwed up tight. Provided it does not create distortion, there is no objection to passing a temporary bolt through the centre of the plate to pull down locally. The hole can quite easily be filled with T.I.G. afterwards.

Where a large number of boats are to be built to a standard design and the hull shape is complex, aluminium is the ideal material for pre-forming. For quantity production, it would pay to indulge in cost cutting methods, even though a considerable investment would be involved in tools and equipment. Bending or shaping plates, or any other part of the structure, for quantity production, can be accomplished in one of three or a combination of the three methods, depending on the complexity of the shape, the size of the section, and the number to be produced. The three methods are:

(1) Pressbrake,
(2) Hydraulic rubber press and
(3) Stretch forming.

(1) No great expenditure is required, if the pressbrake is available. A simple wooden punch and die is used as a top and bottom tool. The aluminium sheet is sandwiched between them and pressure applied. The size of plate and amount of curvature would be somewhat limited, and the tool would have a limited life. Its virtue is simplicity and low cost, but it is not very accurate.

(2) Rubber press work requires considerably more pressure than is normally provided with a press brake. It has a larger, often nearly square rubber bed. Only a punch or top tool is required. The punch presses the aluminium into the rubber, which squeezes it around the punch until it takes the form of the punch. It is sometimes necessary to overbend to allow for springback.

(3) A stretch forming machine is, depending on the size of plate to be worked, very large, powerful, and expensive. The stretch forming operation consists of gripping the sheet tautly at opposite edges, and forcing a form block of the required shape into it. This is usually done in two stages. The sheet is first stressed to just below the yield point, then given an additional stretch to obtain a permanent set. There is very little springback, and the formed parts show little or no distortion. Unlike normal bending, which compresses the metal at the inside of the curve and stretches that on the outside, the stretch former, forms entirely by tension, elongating the metal beyond the elastic limit. This also raises the yield point, so that a stress greater than that originally used to form the shape is required to deform it. Only a great many formed parts would justify initial expenditure, but stretch formers are used in other industries, particularly the aircraft industry, and sometimes time can be hired on a machine. Stretch forming to an appropriate shape can so stiffen a hull that very little internal structure is required. It is possible to form the whole side of a boat in one operation.

For smaller vessels an extruded section at keel, chine, or gunwale can be used (see figure H-2). This has the advantage of trapping and forming a strong edge to the plating, which in turn is welded to it.

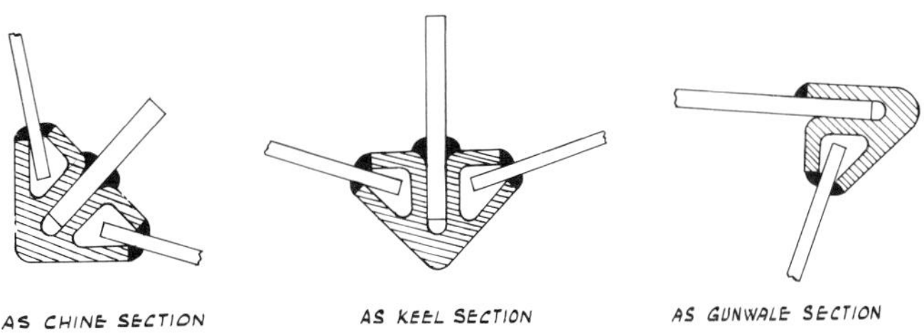

H-2 *Keel and chine section.*

Where a multi-conic design is used, the plating should wrap around the structure without any problem.

Whilst the plating is progressing, it is sometimes an advantage to build in the integral tanks and shaft tunnels, because the welder will have greater access to some otherwise very difficult to get at joints.

If the vessel is built upside down, and spray rails are called for, these should be fully welded in position before turning the boat over.

10 Decking

Decks perform many functions. The scantlings and design must be carefully considered so that areas of high local stress are adequately provided for. The deck forms the upper flange of the main hull girder. It must be watertight to maintain the integrity of the watertight hull, and have permanent or temporary means of closing all openings in the exposed portions. Openings are required for personal access, and in way of machinery spaces to allow removal of machinery when necessary. Other openings with suitable protection are fitted to provide light and air.

Weather decks are normally cambered with a parabolic curve to give added strength and shed water quickly. They may be framed transversely or longitudinally, or as often occurs, a combination of both. Where normally the deck transverses support the longitudinals, longitudinals, frames and deck beams need only be welded intermittently to each other and to underside of deck. Where very high local stresses might occur such as gun mountings or mast steps, a deep transverse immediately under the stress location would be further strengthened with a pillar to a main framing member on the bottom of the hull, consideration must of course be given to the effect this would have on the accommodation below.

Hatch openings should be surrounded by deep coamings with radiused or elliptical corners, in order to reduce stress concentrations. The greatest longitudinal bending stresses occur over the midship region. To accommodate this, the greatest deck plate thickness is maintained over 40% of the length amidships, and tapers to a minimum thickness at the bow and stern.

Decks may be covered with wood sheathing or a plastic deck covering such as Trakmark or Treadmaster. This not only improves the appearance, but provides a non-slip surface, and protection from heat especially in the accommodation areas which can be quite considerable. Direct contact of wood deck to aluminium should be used with discretion, because of the possibility of a slight corrosive effect. This sometimes occurs with oak, and some tropical hardwoods. This can be minimised by bedding the wood onto either a bituminous compound, a butyl rubber compound, or a resin system, which would also act as an adhesive. If it is necessary to secure the wood with through fastenings, these should be counterbored, and the dowels glued.

'Trakmark' and 'Treadmaster' are supplied with their own resin adhesives. These should be applied after the aluminium has been cleaned and degreased.

Bulwarks are often fitted forward. This not only improves the appearance, but gives some personal protection when on the foredeck. These are either an extension of the

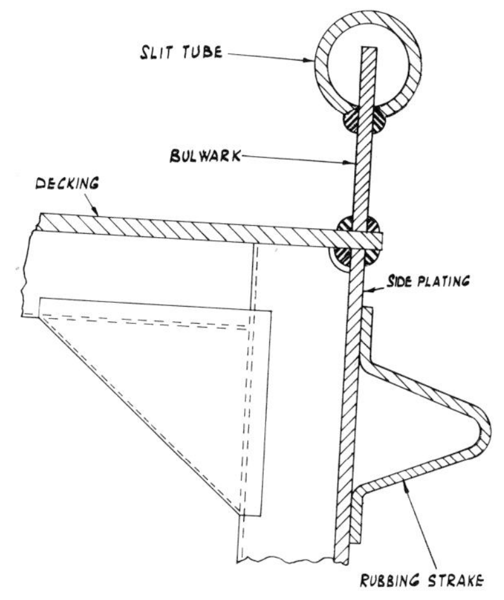

J-1 *Typical bulwark capping.*

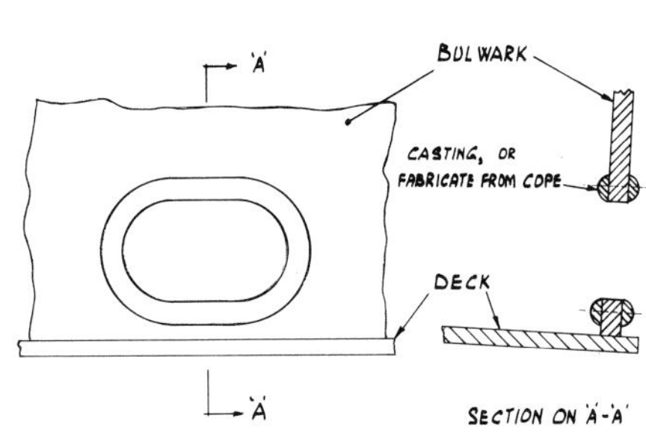

J-2 *Hawse hole ring.*

side plating, or are welded on after the decking margin plate is fitted.

If the bulwarks are tall, they may need stiffening brackets, but usually they are stiff enough by themselves. Should they sustain heavy blows they would probably cause less damage to the deck if brackets are not fitted. The top edge of the bulwark can be protected and stiffened by fitting half round cope, or preferably a split pipe as figure J-1.

Scuppers should be cut at the bottom for drainage, and hawse holes for mooring lines. These, if large, should have some strengthening round the edge. Either a simple sand casting or fabrication. See figure J-2.

11 Superstructures

The design and construction of all deck structures being necessarily prominently positioned, must not only be functional, but aesthetically pleasing. Careful designing can produce a very light and strong structure. Weight saving, particularly above deck level, is a very desirable feature. Overall displacement is reduced with its many benefits, and stability is increased. Aluminium is a very popular material for constructing deck houses, and there are probably more fitted to vessels of every description, than any other single material. It is very common practice to fit aluminium superstructures to steel hulls, and a typical method of securing to the hull is shown in figure K-1. A properly designed shell of, say, 2 or 3 mm., though of adequate strength, can sometimes cause production problems. There are occasions when, because of complex shapes, riveting is not acceptable for appearance or practical reasons. Several rows of rivets on an otherwise unblemished spherical surface are not always pleasing to the eye, especially when each rivet causes a slight flattening under the head. In these circumstances, welding is the only way (see figure K-2).

An experienced welder using the correct procedures, should have little trouble in

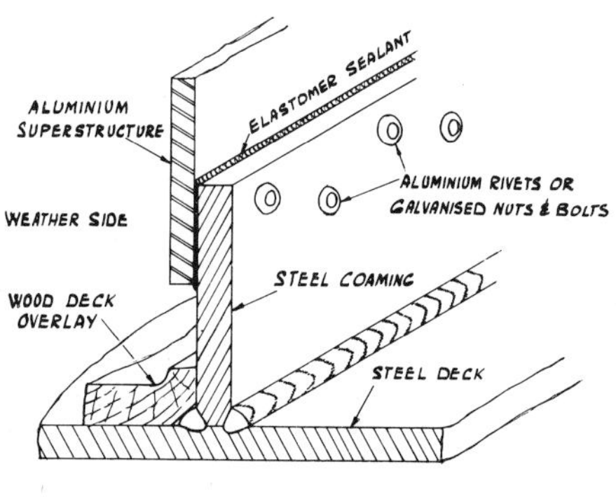

K-1 *Typical method of securing alloy superstructure to steel deck.*

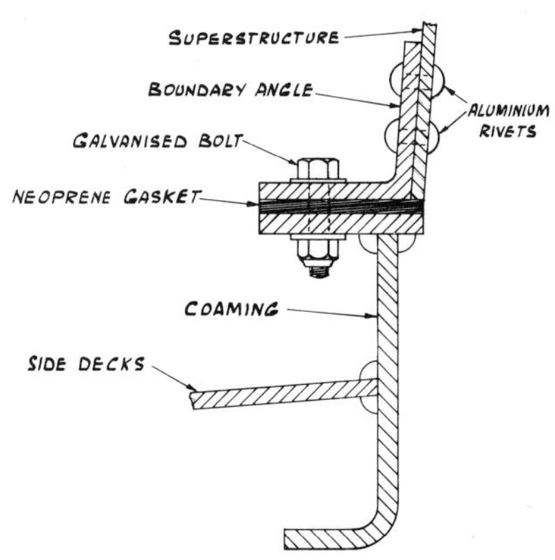

K-2 *Typical method of securing superstructure on all alloy boat.*

producing an acceptable finish. A complex shape will to an extent, assist in resisting distortion. The shell including the stiffening, should be tack welded before full welding is commenced. The window openings should not be cut out until all welding is completed. Depending on operator efficiency, T.I.G. would probably be more suitable. With all the sheets fair, and tack welded in position, final welding can commence. Caution should be observed initially, until a successful technique has been worked out. The following suggestions may help.

Do not overweld—to start with, weld only a few inches at a time.

Do not make an adjacent weld until the first has cooled.

Work alternately port and starboard to equalise contraction stresses. If during the initial tacking the butts were too tight, with insufficient gap, and subsequently distortion is occurring, it may be necessary to cut all the tacks in that butt, and start again with spacers in the seam. It should be appreciated that this type of condition always gets worse as welding proceeds.

Where there are large flat areas, riveting is the obvious choice. Without shape to give rigidity, welding thin gauges would inevitably cause distortion problems. It is possible, however, to combine welding and riveting quite successfully.

Riveted butt joints normally require 4 rows of rivets (2 rows each side staggered). Where this is objected to on grounds of appearance, the butt could be welded, using part of the main structure as a permanent backer.

The centre and perimeter of the panel could then be riveted. The ideal extrusion for interior structure for riveting is a 'zed' section. This provides a riveting flange and an interior stiffening flange, to which linings can be attached, and the intervening space can be filled with insulation. It is not easy to shape 'zeds' and maintain a fair line, so they are restricted to straight lines. If the curves are produced conically, there is of course no problem.

Which type of rivet to use is to some extent a matter of preference, and is discussed more fully in chapter 5 on riveting.

Various fittings such as radio aerials, loud hailers, searchlights, radar scanners, etc. etc., are frequently installed on the wheelhouse roof, often as an afterthought.

It is essential, if the structure is of a light gauge, that local stiffening, commensurate with the load it has carry, should be built in as the erection proceeds.

To secure the deck house in position, it is normal to rivet a ground angle to the base of the structure and bolt this to the deck, or preferably to the coaming around the periphery, with a suitable neoprene type gasket between the mating surfaces, to ensure watertightness. See figure K-3 p. 78.

If the deck house is large, or has a complex shape, it would probably be more advantageous to build it off the boat. This would enable the construction to proceed at the same time as the hull, and it would save a great deal of climbing time. A simple mock up of the deck, or base upon which it will eventually be seated is required, and this can also serve as a base for a jig. Depending to a large extent on the shape or complexity of the deck house, the jig can be in wood, steel, or if a simple shape, the interior structure of the deck house can be erected, and the skin secured directly to it. Where there is a lot of shape, a wooden jig is often more suitable. The panels would be shaped around this, then the interior structure shaped to suit the panels (see fig. K-4).

K-3 *Welded superstructure of complex shape.*

When the superstructure is built off the boat, consideration must be given to lifting it to its final position. It is not always possible or advisable to lift a large structure in one piece. Transport joints should be built into the structure as construction proceeds. These should, wherever possible, be at strong points such as master frames or bulkheads. They will be bolted at watertight pitch with bedding compound on faying surfaces. Lifting lugs can be riveted or bolted, preferably in way of bulkheads.

Care must be exercised so that when lifting, a crushing or squeezing load is not forced upon the structure. This can be avoided by using lifting beams, that will ensure a direct vertical pull on the lifting points. See figure K-5.

When the superstructure is built directly above the engine space, it is necessary to incorporate hatches in the flooring, and the roof of the structure, large enough to allow passage of the engines, both for installation and subsequent removal.

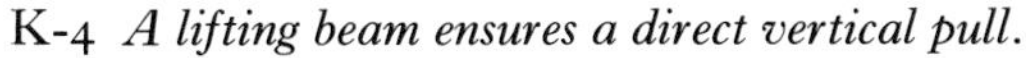
K-4 *A lifting beam ensures a direct vertical pull.*

12 Ancillary Structures

There are an increasing number of economic and functional advantages resulting from the use of aluminium for many marine applications in addition to hull and superstructure.

In the aggregate the weight saving can be considerable, and there is complete compatibility with the aluminium hull. Perhaps more than all other metals, aluminium lends itself to fabrication, provided the proper equipment is available. Much of the material used can be utilised from what would otherwise be scrap. Provided demand exists, and production and distribution costs are reasonable, a production-orientated company could well add considerably to their gross income with little additional capital investment. Besides producing marine items such as boat hardware, electrical equipment, plumbing, furniture, ducting, dock and harbour structures etc., household equipment, office furniture, partitions, air conditioning equipment, ladders, portable garden furniture, parts for motor cars and many other items could be produced. The combination of light weight and corrosion resistance, coupled with ease of fabrication, makes the prospect worthy of consideration.

We are, however, concerned here only with those items that have a direct application to boatbuilding, some of which are hereunder detailed:

Masts and spars

Apart from the normal round tube extrusions, there are many other special mast extrusions available. Some with internal or external integral sail tracks. With a little judicious vee shaped cutting and welding, these can be tapered to reduce weight and windage. They can also be formed on a brakepress or roll formed. Extruded mast tracks can be added externally. Some typical shapes are shown in figure L-1. Aluminium lugs and cleats may be cast or cut from sheet or extruded sections for attaching standing and running rigging. It is normal to anodise the spars after manufacture. This provides a lasting and pleasing finish, no other treatment being required.

Tanks

Fuel and water tanks are frequently made of aluminium regardless of the hull

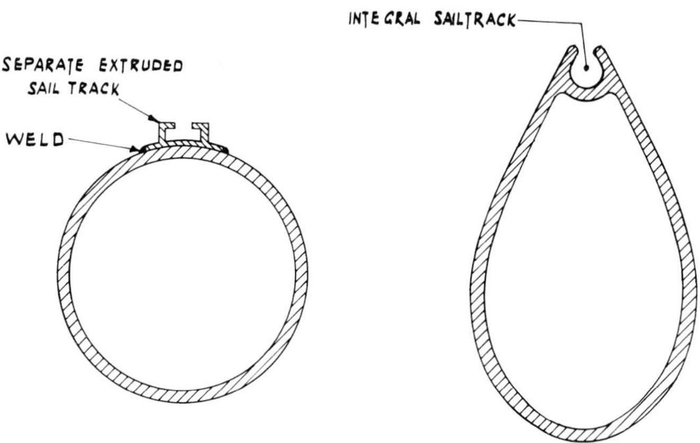

L-1 *Typical mast extrusions.*

material. The interior of fuel tanks, diesel and petrol, are often left unpainted. Fresh water tanks are sometimes treated internally with a special composition to reduce the possibility of a slightly tainted taste over a period of years. Sewage and sanitary tanks, particularly if they are integral, should be coated internally with a bitumastic solution such as 'Proderite'. There is a possibility of a corrosive effect setting up an action over a long period if the metal is left bare.

Ladders

Special hollow extrusions are produced for ladders or they can be fabricated from plate and tube. Unless quantity production is envisaged, it would probably be uneconomic to set up a production process. Purchasing from specialist manufacturers who produce in very large numbers, normally at a very economic price, would probably prove cheaper.

Watertight doors

These are normally quite straightforward and could very easily be produced by the boatbuilders. Swages are often formed in the door panel to provide the same strength with lighter gauge material. Handles can be fabricated or be simple sand castings. A typical section is shown in figure L-2 p. 82.

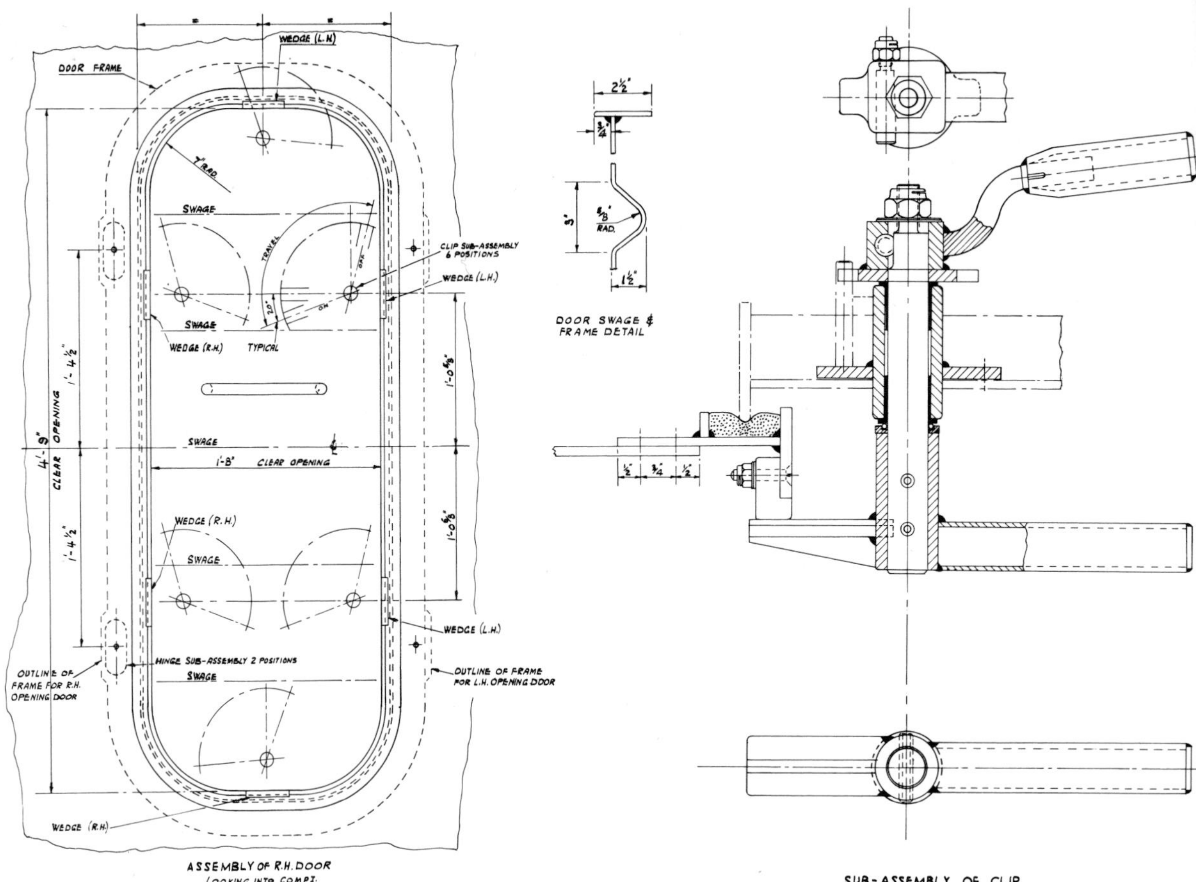

L-2 *Arrangement of watertight door.*

Window frames

Many extruded sections are produced for the various types of windows; fixed, half drop, sliding and hinged. Radius corners are formed on special-purpose tooling and mitred corners are welded. Weather seals can also be obtained for fitting into the fixed or sliding type frames. These may be silicone-treated wool-pile seals, polyethylene guides or vinyl weatherstripping. See figure L-3.

Wherever possible, safety glass should be installed in the frames, particularly if they are large, and/or forward facing. It is sometimes necessary to accept plastic glazing for curved frames. This is not really desirable as the plastic is normally a good deal softer than glass and more susceptible to scratches, which in time tend to obscure vision. Where the vessel is intended to be used in the Mediterranean or eastern waters where

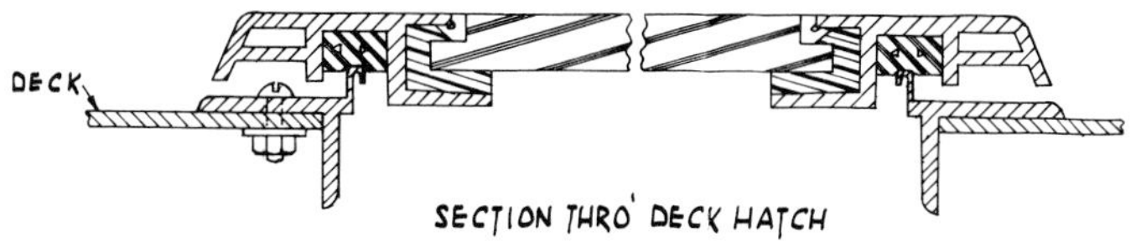

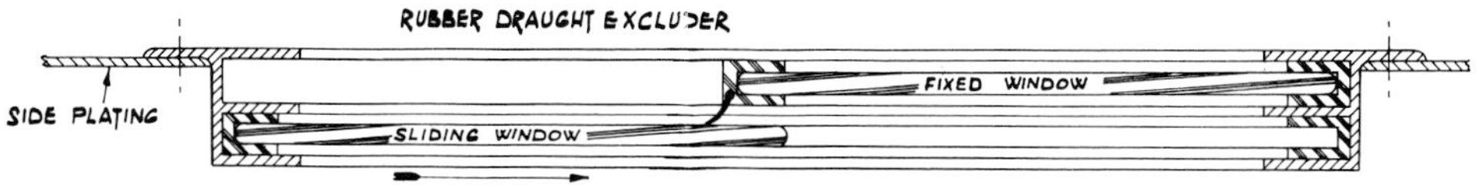

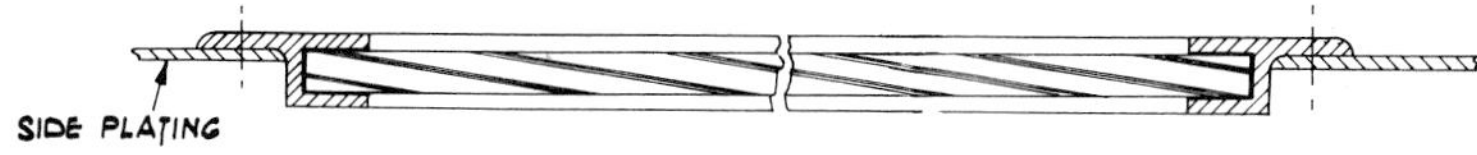

L-3 *Weather seals.*

L-4 *Aluminium sheet brackets for windscreens.*

sunlight is particularly bright, it is highly recommended to use a tinted glass such as I.C.I. 911. This, whilst not obstructing vision, reduces glare and heat penetration. All frames should be anodised to retain their bright appearance.

Windscreens or windshields arranged as a protection on the external flying bridge, may have brackets very simply fabricated from aluminium sheet similar to that shown in figure L-4. Where the eye level is above the top of the screen, these may be in plastic such as acrylic or perspex. They would be considerably cheaper than glass and when damaged, more easily replaced. Opening portlights and deadlight frames are usually castings and are available in many shapes, sizes and types. Unless the required item is not obtainable from suppliers, it is probably cheaper to purchase them.

Deck fittings

A very wide variety are obtainable from many marine factors. For items such as fairleads, cleats and bollards, where a high quality yacht finish is required, these are probably best purchased as castings. They can be very expensive if supplied with a highly polished finish. If a cheaper fitting is preferred, they can sometimes be obtained from the foundry in an 'as cast' condition. These are fairly smooth, but of course lack the brilliance of a polished surface. They would normally be acceptable on commercial or service craft. Where an even cheaper fitting is required, these can be fabricated quite cheaply from offcuts of tube and plate, as in figure L-5.

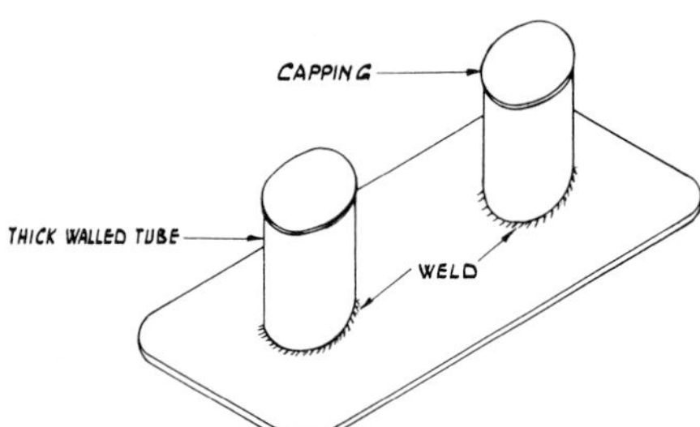

L-5 *Fabricated bollards.*

Deck fillers with screwed caps are readily available as castings to suit from 1 in. to 2 in. pipe. For sizes outside this range, tube and plate welded would be satisfactory but the screwed filler cap would have to be fairly thick to allow for the thread and deck key.

Handrails are simply made from tube, with the fittings, sockets and brackets, either castings or fabrications.

Side deck stanchions are made from tube with the top blanked off, and where wire rope passes through the stanchion, a small insert tube should be welded in to eliminate chaffing of the wire. Deck stanchion sockets, where a number are required, should be obtained as castings. If less than about ten are required, tube welded onto plate would suffice. A drain hole should be drilled close to the base and a drop nose pin with keep chain secures the stanchion in the socket.

Hawse pipes that pass through the deck as leads for the anchor chain, and anchor, are fabricated from large tube, to suit the individual requirement. The end of the tube that secures to the stem or side plate should have a heavy reinforcement to withstand the chain wear. A typical example is illustrated in figure L-6.

Ventilators of the cowl type are normally pressed into shape or spun, and beyond the scope of the average boatbuilder. Mushroom ventilators could be produced by the

L-6 *Prefabricated hawse pipe.*

boatbuilder but unless they were fairly large, above 6 in. diameter, would not be economical to produce in small numbers.

Aluminium ducting for air conditioning is almost the standard, irrespective of hull material. Light weight, easy formability and resistance to the effect of moisture which is inevitably present in the system, make it ideal.

Boxes containing all the electrical control switch gear, fuses, distributors, rectifiers, transformers, circuit breakers, etc., and instrument panels for the various meters and switches, are very easily produced with the aid of a folder. Aluminium, being non-magnetic, can be used in close proximity with the magnetic compass, without any deviation effect.

Aluminium fuel piping, fresh water piping and bilge pipes are frequently installed. Joints are easily made with cone nuts, or flanged joints. Small diameter pipes up to about $\frac{1}{2}$ in. diameter are easily bent around a hand former without filling. Larger diameters require filling with 'Sarabend' or similar to prevent kinking.

Deck boxes for the stowage of ropes, fendoffs etc., and many other applications can very easily be formed, and riveted or welded often from otherwise scrap, in this most versatile of all materials.

13 Painting

Painting has two general functions to perform: (1) protection and (2) cosmetic. Of the two, protection is the more important, as this may well affect the life and service of the vessel.

Protective coatings

These can also be broken down under two headings: (a) protection against electrolytic action by the proximity of dissimilar metals, and (b) protection of the ship's underwater plating by fouling of natural marine growth.

(a) *Electrolytic action*

As explained in chapter 14 on corrosion, two dissimilar metals in an electrolyte will tend to set up an electric cell and the more active or anodic metal will want to disintegrate. Among the ways of preventing this from causing real harm, is to fit sacrificial anodes. This, though, is only really necessary where an electrolyte—e.g., seawater, is present, normally on the outside of the hull. There are other places; inside the hull and topsides which will also need protection, for although the effect is greatest directly in seawater, a salt atmosphere can also have an effect. A suitable paint scheme will very effectively isolate the two surfaces and whilst intact, will eliminate or minimise any trouble.

It is very good practice that all faying (mating) surfaces should have an insulating layer between them. This will isolate the surfaces and prevent the entrapment of moisture. The insulating material must be inert and suitable for the function it has to perform.

Where an aluminium skin fitting is through bolted to the skin or bulkhead, a thin layer of P.R.C. jointing compound (already described in chapter 5 on fastenings) or similar, should be sandwiched between the two surfaces and around the bolt head and shank. Where it is necessary to pass copper piping, or similar cathodic material through an aluminium bulkhead as is sometimes called for, as for instance in some air conditioning installations carrying refrigerants, the piping should pass through the bulkhead as high up as possible away from the bilge, and a rubber or neoprene gasket should isolate the copper from the aluminium.

(b) *Anti-fouling*

The surface waters of the sea contain immense numbers of floating microscopic animal and plant life, known generally as plankton. Among the plankton are innumerable young or 'larva' forms of such creatures as barnacles, mussels, etc., which, when grown up, are found attached to objects below the surface. The plankton also contains millions of spores of various seaweeds.

All vessels in the sea are, therefore, immersed in this collection of living organisms, a great many of which will settle, if they get the chance, on their hulls and grow into a fouling growth. Although these various forms of growth cannot directly harm the aluminium hull, they can if left unchecked, result in a serious loss of speed, and by masking the sacrificial anodes, and destroying the paint scheme, could, where dissimilar metals are present, lead to corrosion of the hull. To prevent this fouling of the bottom, it is strongly recommended to coat with an anti-fouling composition. The principle underlying the use of anti-fouling compositions is that as the toxic substances which they contain slowly and constantly dissolve, the ship's surface is permanently surrounded by a thin layer of toxic solution. Therefore, if the anti-fouling is functioning properly—i.e., if the toxic layer is being maintained, the marine growth will be prevented from obtaining a foothold. The fouling attack always comes from organisms in a microscopic condition, and if the film of water in immediate contact with the ship's surface can be kept in a condition toxic to this primitive life, the organisms are destroyed.

The anti-fouling film is, therefore, a store for poisonous materials which are constantly being dissolved by the sea. The poisons in most common use today are derived from copper, mercury, and tin. In addition, some specialised anti-foulings may contain other forms of organic poisons. No paint or composition containing mercury or copper should ever be used on aluminium, even over protective coatings. Mercury is specially dangerous, as it inhibits the formation of a protective coating of oxide and without this the alloy can rapidly erode. Many paint manufacturers produce a composition that is especially suitable for aluminium. Their advice should be sought and a full paint scheme, including suitable undercoats, applied.

One other form of anti-fouling should be mentioned—tank interiors. Fuel tanks do not need painting.

Fresh water tanks should always be etched and painted because, over a period of time, fresh water containing certain contaminates can cause a slime to adhere to the aluminium.

This does not harm the aluminium, but it may cause the taste to be affected. Sanitary and sewage tanks should also be treated, as this can have a corrosive effect; here again, paint manufacturers should be consulted for suitable coatings for each situation.

Decorative painting

The topsides of an aluminium hull need be painted only for appearance sake. If left bare, a dirty matt-grey finish will result, and a white powder will form on the surface. This is a self-protecting salt-like structure that is inherent in the aluminium, and will cause no harm.

Aluminium holds paint well, provided the surface is properly prepared for receiving the ground coats and is applied in thicknesses and under conditions recommended by the paint manufacturer. Most of them suggest that the ideal temperature for painting is between 60 and 80°F., with relative humidity between 30 and 40%. Regardless of the kind of paint, under high humidity conditions the temperature of the hull should be higher than that of the surrounding air, to prevent condensation. No painting should be done outside after sundown if it is possible for dew to form, and, of course, never in a damp atmosphere.

Here is a typical painting specification with materials supplied by International Yacht Paints:

Description of materials

Self-etch primer

Light alloy and galvanised zinc may have a greasy and highly polished surface that must be pre-treated before painting. They must first be de-greased and then coated with self-etch primer which, in one operation, etches the surface and provides the protective coat. Self-etching primer and its accelerator are supplied separately. Two parts self-etching primer to one part accelerator should be mixed immediately before application and used within eight hours.

The mixture should be applied as a thin wash coat, approximately 13.0 sq.m/litre. It is important to note the colour change which takes place after some minutes, indicating that the material has 'taken'. Under no circumstances should a second coat be applied.

Drying time—4 hours.
Apply light alloy primer or metallic primocon 4–24 hours later.
Covering capacity—13.0 sq.m./litre.

Light alloy primer

Light alloy primer is a corrosion inhibitor and is used over self-etch primer, except below the water line outside.

Drying time—4 to 6 hours.
Interval between coats—1 to 10 days.
Covering capacity—10 sq.m./litre.

Metallic primocon

Metallic primocon is used on all under water surfaces and is compatible with the surface of anti-fouling. The anti-fouling must be applied direct to the primocon.

Drying time—4 hours.
Interval between coats—1 day to 3 weeks.
Covering capacity—12 sq.m./litre.

T.B.T. anti-fouling

Especially produced for use on light alloy craft. Should be immersed within 6 weeks of first application.

Surface drying time—1 hour.
Interval between coats—6 to 24 hours.
Covering capacity—9.8 sq.m./litre.
Special thinners No. 3.

Water tank black

Care to be taken before application to see that surfaces are perfectly clean and dry. While the paint is being applied, adequate ventilation must be maintained throughout the drying period. Before the tank is put into use, thoroughly flush with fresh water.

Drying time—about 6 hours.
Covering capacity—10 sq.m./litre.

Painting Procedure

Exterior hull bottom

(1) Clean all welds and weld penetration marks. Burnish total area with graded emery cloth.
(2) De-grease with Acetone or Maritec.
(3) Apply one coat self-etch primer.
(4) After 16 to 24 hours, apply one coat metallic primocon.
(5) At about 24 hour intervals, apply a further four coats metallic primocon.
(6) After five days, apply first coat T.B.T. anti-fouling.
(7) After between 6 to 24 hours, apply second coat T.B.T. anti-fouling.

NOTE: most important

The following must be masked prior to, and not painted:

(a) Sacrificial anodes.
(b) Propellers.
(c) Propeller shafts.

Exterior hull topsides and superstructures

(1) Clean all welds, and weld penetration marks, but do not totally remove weld beads. Burnish total area with graded emery cloth.
(2) De-grease with Acetone or Maritec.
(3) Apply one coat self-etch primer.
(4) After 16 to 24 hours, apply one coat light alloy primer.
(5) Face up irregularities with trowel cement.
(6) After 16 to 24 hours, apply second coat light alloy primer.
(7) After 16 to 24 hours, apply first coat undercoat.
(8) After 16 to 24 hours, apply second coat undercoat.
(9) After 16 to 24 hours, apply first coat enamel.
(10) After 16 to 24 hours, rub down lightly with fine grade emery.
(11) Apply second coat enamel.

Decks

For areas that are not covered with special deck covering such as 'Treadmaster', paint as for topsides, but final coat should be either non-slip deck paint, or non-slip grit should be added.

Engine room

(1) For areas that are covered with insulation, no painting is required, and do not paint the insulation.
(2) Flooring treadplate should not be painted.
(3) Underfloor areas need not be painted.
(4) All other exposed areas may be coated with a fire retardant paint.

Accommodation

(1) Plywood linings—bulkheads—partitions—overheads.
(a) Rub down thoroughly to all surfaces.
(b) Apply one coat aluminium wood primer.
(c) Apply two coats undercoat at intervals of 24 hours.
(d) To overheads apply two coats matt finish at intervals of 24 hours.
(e) To sides, apply two coats enamel at intervals of 24 to 48 hours.
(2) Mahogany trim
(a) Rub down thoroughly to all surfaces.
(b) Apply one coat 20% turpentine and varnish.
(c) At intervals of between 24 to 48 hours, apply four coats of varnish.

NOTE: rub down lightly between each coat of paint or varnish to produce smooth even finish.

Fresh water tank interior
(1) De-grease.
(2) Apply one coat self-etch primer.
(3) After 16 to 24 hours, apply one coat water tank black.

Whether to apply the paint by brush, roller, or spray, will depend very largely on the custom of the yard and skills of the operators. Brushing would probably be more convenient for small enclosed areas, and spraying for large areas. Where spraying is used, adjacent areas must be masked against overspray.

The type of topcoat to be used; enamel, acrylics, polyurethanes, or epoxide resin compositions, will depend on the job and life required. The paint manufacturers should be consulted for your own special requirements.

14 Corrosion

Corrosion of metals is an electro-chemical reaction in which the metals react to become oxides or salts. That is a tendency to return to the ore from which the metal was obtained originally.

In electrical terms, the process involves the loss of electrons from the metallic atom. This means a tiny electrical current is flowing away from the metal. Different metals have a varying electrical potential and the following table shows their relative positions:

Most active	Magnesium
	Zinc
	Galvanised mild steel
	Aluminium
	Iron
	Steel
	Tin
	Lead
	Brass
	Copper
	Silver
Least active	Gold

When two metals are placed in an electrolyte, e.g., seawater, and connected electrically, a current will pass from the more active to the least active, due to their different electrical potentials. If the current is sufficiently strong, the less active metal

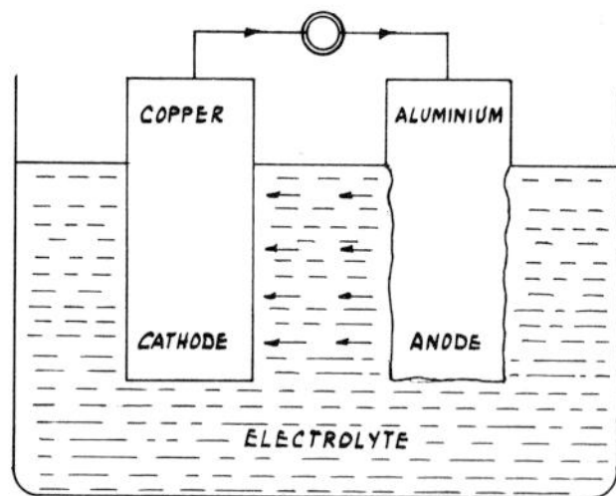

M-1 *Galvanic corrosion.*

will cease corroding: in electrical terms it is cathodic to the more active metal, which as the giver of the current, is called the anode. In releasing this current, the anode will slowly disintegrate and go into solution. A simple galvanic cell in which a small electric current is passing from the aluminium anode to the copper cathode is illustrated in figure M-1.

Galvanic cell

A single piece of metal may become anodic at one point and cathodic at another. Eventually, a hole will appear at the anode where metal has gone into solution, current flowing towards the cathodic area. The phenomenon is due usually to microscopic impurities or discontinuities in the metal. If a pin hole is left in the coating on a metal surface, particularly rapid corrosion can occur at this point.

The sacrificial anode

Anodes both in size and composition vary in strict relation to the job they have to perform. It is the expert's job to advise on the material, shape, and size, and positioning of the anodes in relation to all other underwater fittings.

The anode chosen will always be electro-negative to the metal it has to protect, and will, therefore, attract the electric currents present, and corrode first. It is not easy to calculate with accuracy the wasting rate of the anode. It should, therefore, be examined at least every six months for the early part of the vessel's life.

Relative areas of cathode and anode are usually as important as, and related to potential differences. The combination of a large anode, say an aluminium hull, and a small cathode, say a manganese bronze propeller, even if not in direct electrical contact, can cause corrosion if the shaft is not also electrically isolated.

It is not always necessary to have dissimilar metals for the creation of these destructive currents. Potential differences can be set up by turbulence and differential aeration, particularly with planing hulls. This must not, of course, be confused with cavitation, which is another subject entirely,

The ideal situation would be to have all underwater fittings of the same metal, and then there would be little trouble from corrosion. At the moment this is not possible but there are many things that can be done to ease the situation. Sea cocks can now be obtained in aluminium, and plastic. Shaft bearings can be rubber encased in a hard plastic or stainless steel shell, so insulating the shaft from the hull. All underwater fittings and through fastenings should be of compatible material and bedded down on a suitable bedding compound. A full and proper paint scheme should be applied, together with a suitable anti-fouling. No paint containing mercury or copper should ever be used. Several paint manufacturers produce an anti-fouling especially suitable for aluminium. When painting underwater, the sacrificial anodes must not, of course, be painted, as this does inhibit their use. There are many cases where alloy fittings such as window frames, have corroded very badly. Often this is not due to electrolytic action, but to the use of an alloy unsuitable to withstand the chemical action of salt spray.

Internal electric currents can also be a source of corrosion. These can be guarded against by the correct installation and insulation of all wiring and auxiliary motors. The installation of the D.C. current system should be fully insulated with an earth return wire and not earthed through the hull, otherwise any fault in the system could cause a current to pass through the hull, and create a corrosion problem.

If precautions are not taken, corrosion can become a major problem, but this need not be so. If it is recognised as a potential problem at the design stage, and the appropriate action taken by seeking advice from a competent authority, the problem can be reduced to minimal proportions, The points raised in this book, have, by necessity, been of a general nature, and each vessel requires a separate study.

In considering this problem, one has to think of the effect over a period of years, This, then, makes the solution so much more desirable and worthwhile.

15 Sterngear

The term 'sterngear' is here intended to cover those normal external underwater items in power craft that contribute to turning and motion. It includes rudders, tailshafts, shaft brackets, and propellers.

The type, design, and material depend to a large extent on the power, speed, size and function of the vessel. The materials should, insofar as it is possible, be compatible with the aluminium hull. It is often necessary to make a compromise between compatibility, and strength of material.

A copper base material, though not desirable, can be used with discretion, provided the ratio of the area of the cathodic material (copper) is insignificant compared with that of the anodic material (aluminium), and provided they are physically separated, and sacrificial plates are fitted.

Tailshafts are often one of the stainless steels, preferably the 18/8 'Austenitic' type. The strength of this material is not very great (about 35 U.T.S.) and when a stronger material is required, either one of the 'Aquamet' or 'Monel' metals is used. These have a very much greater strength factor, and by careful selection can be reasonably compatible.

Shaft brackets, when required as a casting, will normally be in a cast steel. The specification of the material depending on the strength factors required. For a high speed craft, requiring the minimum cross sectional area, a manganese steel could be used. The bearing in the bracket would be of the rubber 'cutless' type, bonded to a plastic or stainless steel outer shell, and not the more usual brass type outer shell.

Where a smaller diameter shaft (1.5 in. or less) is sufficient with moderate horse power (up to about 50 B.H.P.), a simple arrangement with plate and tube could be used, similar to that illustrated in figure N-1 p. 96.

'Tufnol' or 'Lignum Vitae' bearings may be used, provided a natural flow of water can be maintained for lubrication. Where the vessel is normally used in sand or grit laden waters, a rubber bearing is considered superior and longer lasting.

Rudders. For the larger faster craft, the blades will probably be in cast steel similar to the shaft brackets, with a stainless steel stock. The interior stock and bearing housings being cast aluminium, similar to the illustration in fig. N-2 p. 97. For the smaller slower craft, a stainless steel stock with either stainless steel or aluminium plate blade, as illustrated in fig. N-3 p. 98. There are, of course, a great many variations of blade shape and size. The variables determining this being speed of craft, cost, power, whether twin engined and twin rudders, underwater shape of hull, displace-

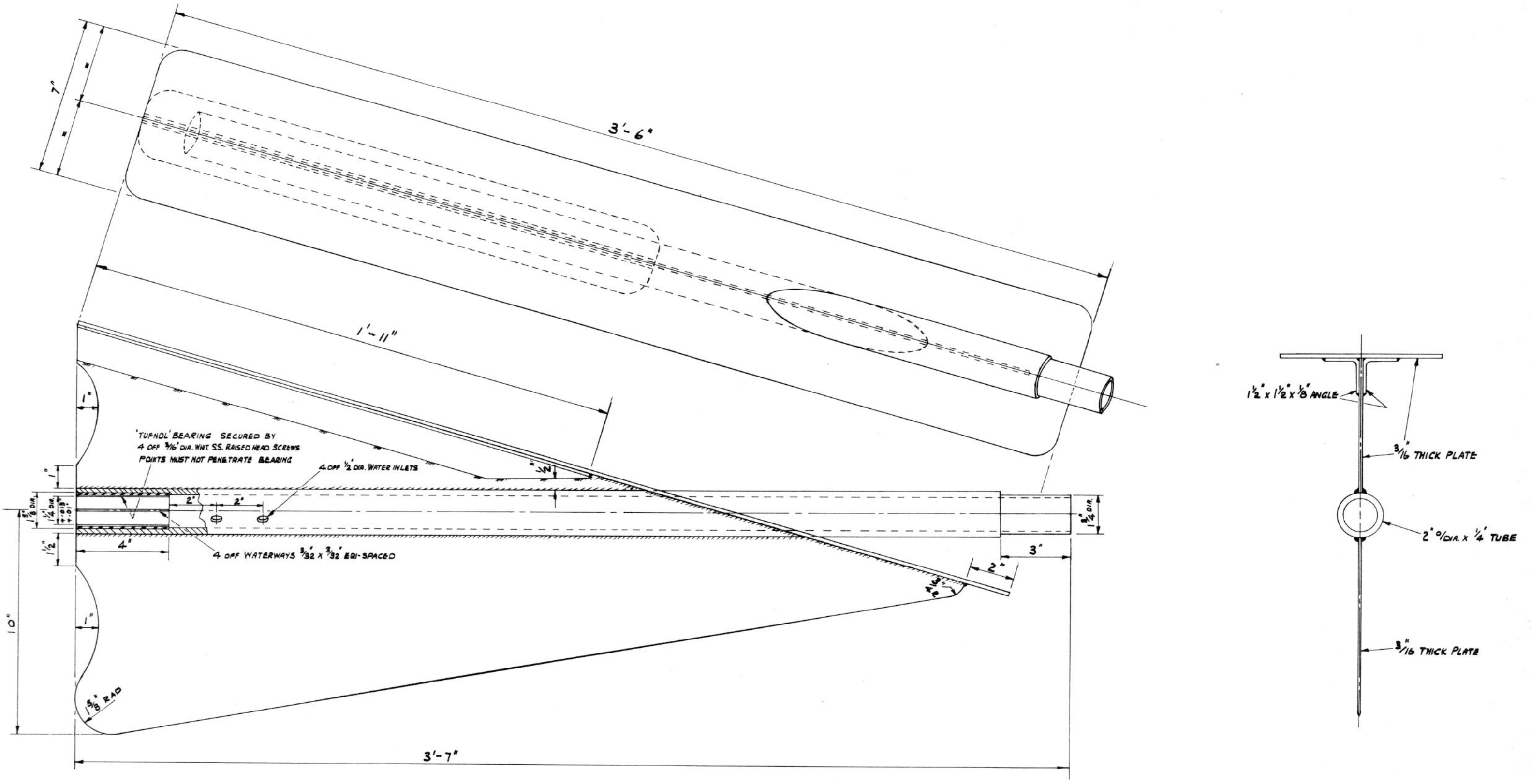

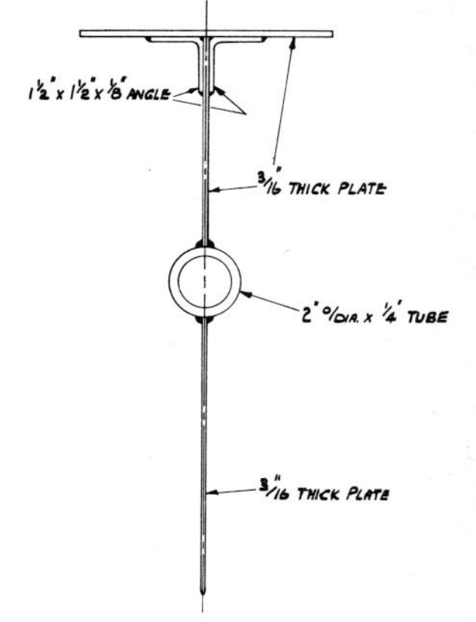

N-1 *Sterntube for small craft.*

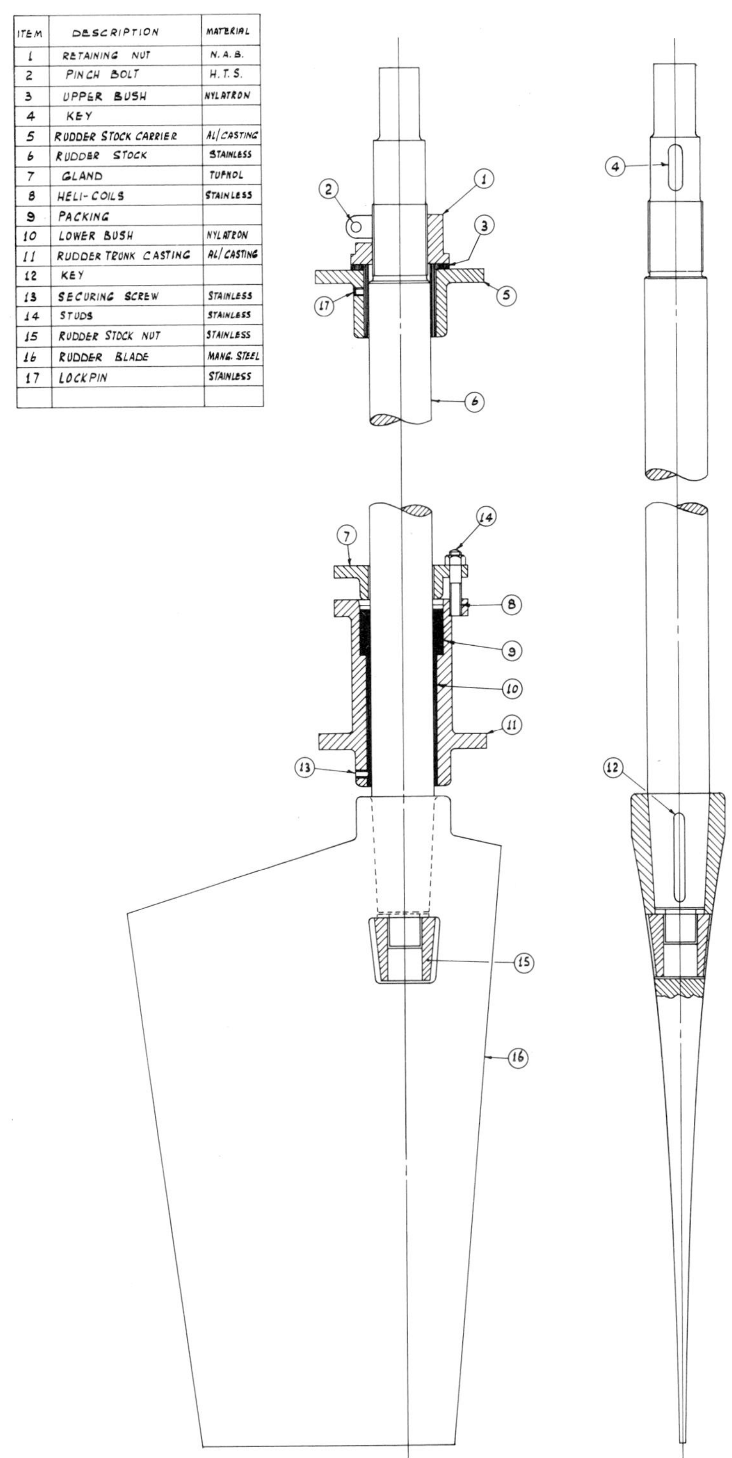

ITEM	DESCRIPTION	MATERIAL
1	RETAINING NUT	N. A. B.
2	PINCH BOLT	H. T. S.
3	UPPER BUSH	NYLATRON
4	KEY	
5	RUDDER STOCK CARRIER	AL/CASTING
6	RUDDER STOCK	STAINLESS
7	GLAND	TUFNOL
8	HELI-COILS	STAINLESS
9	PACKING	
10	LOWER BUSH	NYLATRON
11	RUDDER TRUNK CASTING	AL/CASTING
12	KEY	
13	SECURING SCREW	STAINLESS
14	STUDS	STAINLESS
15	RUDDER STOCK NUT	STAINLESS
16	RUDDER BLADE	MANG. STEEL
17	LOCKPIN	STAINLESS

N-2 *Rudder for 75 ft. patrol boat.*

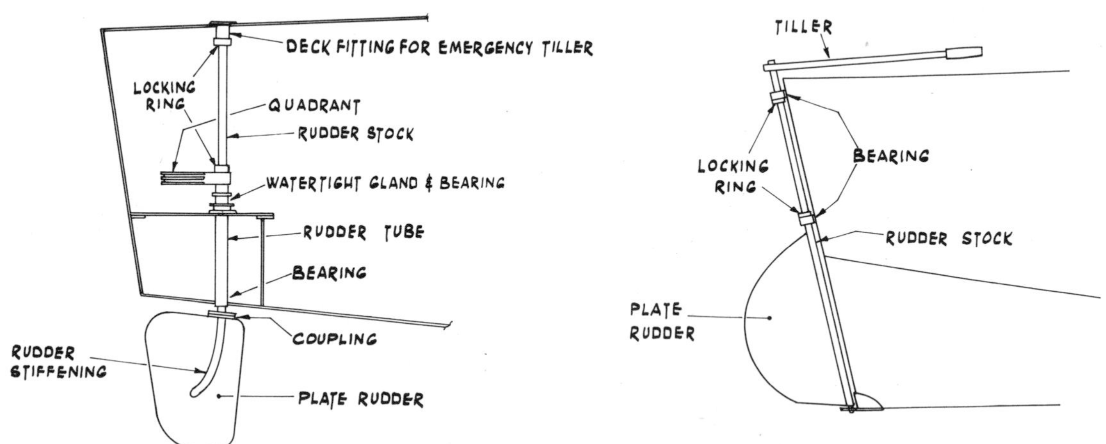

N-3 *Sterngear for medium power small craft.*

N-4 *Rudder blade for sailing boat.*

ment, and material. A sailing vessel will have an entirely different blade shape and area, and may well be hung on the transom as fig. N-4 p. 98.
Propellers. For small craft, with engines up to about 200 B.H.P., a Z-drive transom unit is ideal, because the leg, which includes steering and propeller, is of aluminium alloy, and normally compatible with an aluminium hull.

Stainless steel in one of its various forms and specifications is also a good propeller material. When bronze propellors must be used, chromium plating will tend to minimise corrosion problems. When the vessel is not normally afloat when not in use, or when used only in fresh water, the problem of dissimilar metals is not so great, and the restrictions so imposed can with discretion be relaxed.

16 Fitting Out

The arrangement and assembly of accommodation areas is little different in an aluminium hull to any other form of hull structure. Where the interior fit out and linings are of wood, wood grounds are usually secured to the aluminium frames. Fastenings would usually be of galvanised mild steel. A metal hull will, under certain climatic conditions, suffer more from condensation than a wooden hull. It will also retain more heat and transmit sound. For this and other reasons it is advisable to insulate against heat and sound transference, particularly if the vessel has accommodation areas.

It is essential that insulations in the engine room and any other machinery spaces shall be particularly fire proof and completely incombustible. The purpose for which the vessel is designed will, to some extent, dictate the extent to which the insulation shall be fire proof. In passenger vessels built to classification, especially stringent fire precautions are laid down.

There are many materials available that will provide both accoustic and thermal insulation. These can be divided into two main groups; rigid or semi-rigid panels, and spraying in situ.

The rigid panels are supplied as 'navy board', asbestos, polyurethane, rock wool, 'Dampa', 'Limpet' boards etc. Some of them are intended for application as free standing bulkheads, linings and ceilings, and have decorative finishings bonded to the exterior. Semi-rigid panels can be obtained as rockwool, glass wool, mineral wool etc., the different types offering varying insulating properties. They can also be obtained in thicknesses from 1 in. to 4 in. depending on the degree of insulation. They must be supported, often being fitted between structural members, and faced with a rigid lining. A typical engine room arrangement is shown in figure P-1 p. 100.

Spray insulation is marketed under several trade names. The more usual types have as their base either asbestos or polyurethane. Specialist firms with their own pump and spray units visit the vessel and, using their own specialist labour, will spray directly on to the interior any thickness required. It is advisable to etch prime (see painting chapter) the effected area prior to spraying. This provides a key for better adhesion, and reduces the possibility of interaction with the aluminium due to contaminants in the spraying material. The polyurethane type material is a two-component admix, which produces a foaming reaction when mixed on spraying. A good deal of overspraying takes place, so it is advisable to mask areas not to be sprayed. It is very light in weight but care must be taken that the material is fireproof and not

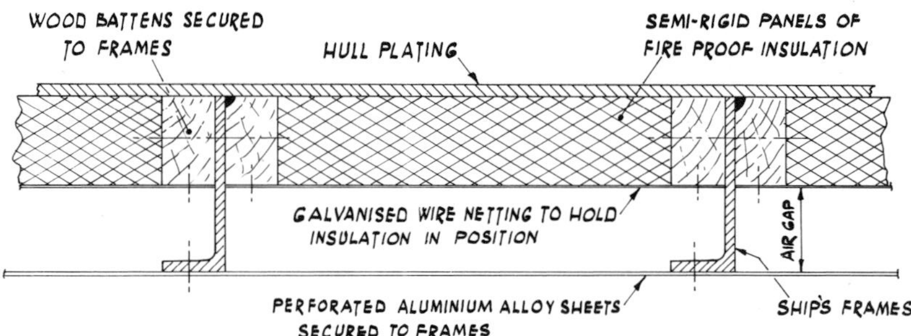

P-1 *Fitting of insulation panels in larger engine room.*

capable of giving off noxious fumes when subjected to flame.

The asbestos material is proof against fire, is a good deal heavier, does not have the same sound proofing qualities, and could be more of a health hazard if the necessary precautions are not taken against disintegration, and contamination.

All vessels, large and small, sail and power, should be protected against a fire hazard. The degree of protection will to a large extent depend upon the degree of risk. The high risk areas demand the greatest protection. Wherever highly combustible fuels are used, there is need for protection.

There are various types of extinguishant, many being produced for dealing with a specific type of fire; Class A (carbonaceous material), Class B (flammable liquids) and Class C (electrical equipment). When used, they discharge a powder, gas, liquid or foam.

On the smaller vessels, a few hand extinguishers located at strategic points would normally be adequate. On the larger vessels a more sophisticated system should be considered.

In the high risk areas; engine room etc., a ring main consisting of stainless steel piping strategically positioned above and below the flooring, with holes drilled at intervals directed at high risk points, is connected to the extinguishant container. The container can be discharged by mechanical/manual operation remotely, or by automatic electrical means.

It is usual when the vessel is manned, to switch the discharge to manual operation; this reduces the risk of accidental discharge, and to switch to automatic when the vessel is unmanned.

Fire sensors are positioned strategically, and connected electrically to a warning alarm and automatic control.

The extinguishant used in these systems is usually an all-purpose type, either CO_2 or Bromochlorodifluoromethane (B.C.F.).

Another often overlooked hazard is the explosive gas given off from batteries that are being charged. In the majority of larger vessels, several banks of batteries providing light and power are being continually charged when the main or auxiliary engines are operating. This can result in an accumulation of gases that should be discharged to the outside atmosphere. Where forced ventilation is used, and this is very desirable, special spark proof gas extraction fans should be incorporated in the trunking. A typical installation is illustrated in figure P-2.

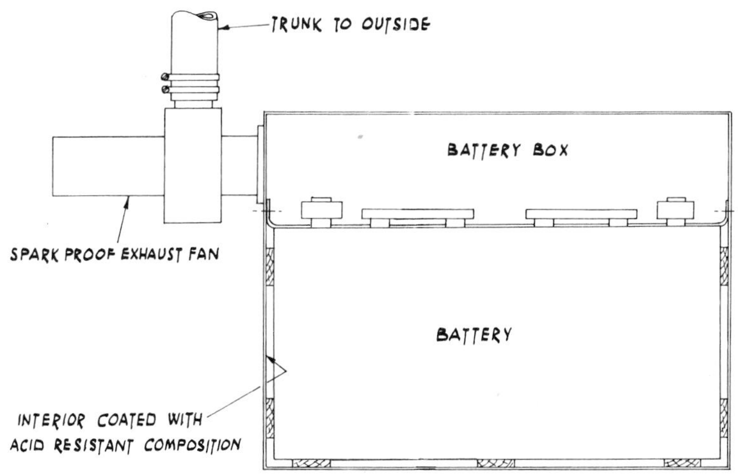

P-2 *Battery installation.*

17 Launching

With the vessel nearly completed, it has to be transferred to the water. This can be done in one of six different ways; (1) dry dock, (2) sideways launching, (3) slippery ways, (4) cradle, (5) slings around the boat and (6) gunwale plates and slings.

Dry dock

If the vessel is built in a dry dock, it is then only necessary to flood the dock. Normally only very large vessels are launched in this way and it is most unlikely that the type of vessel under consideration would ever be launched in this way.

Sideways launching

The vessel is placed on a framework sideways on, and close to the quay from which it is to be launched. The side of the framework furthest from the water is lifted by jacks or other means. The vessel will then slide into the water, or inertia can be overcome by the application of force on the side by further jacks. This method is usually only used when launching into a narrow river, or where there is no slipway or lifting gear.

Slippery ways

Launching ways are set up, either on a slipway or on an inclined plane, consisting of a fixed portion on the ground, and a sliding portion attached to the vessel. Between the two portions is a layer of thick grease. Initially, the sliding portion is held in position by 'dogs' which, upon being released, allow the vessel to slide into the water (see figure Q-1).

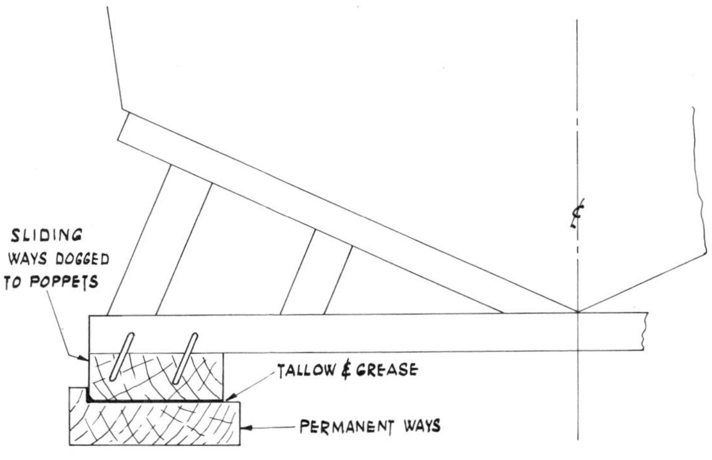

Q-1 *Slippery ways.*

Cradle

This consists of a well braced steel framework, in one or more sections, usually set on wheels. A slipway is necessary, leading into the water. Metal rails are usually set into the slipway to receive the wheels on the cradle. These wheels may be fixed (non-swivelling) where the cradle is used only on the slipway or in a straight line, or castored (swivelling) when the cradle is used to transport the vessel around the yard. If the cradle is in one section only, it should be at least one third the length of the vessel, and preferably longer, with poppets supporting the vessel placed at strategic points—i.e., in way of strength members such as bulkheads, or deep frames (see fig. Q-2 p. 104).

When launching into tidal waters, the cradle could be placed on the lower section of the slipway at low water, and when the tide rises, the boat will float off. Discretion should be used with larger vessels because of the extra stress imposed in way of the forward poppet when the stern starts to lift. In vessels with a strong girder-like structure such as engine beds extending all fore and aft and numerous stringers and reasonably calm weather conditions, no problems should be encountered. Where there is a doubt, a naval architect should be consulted. A few simple calculations will indicate the degree of risk involved.

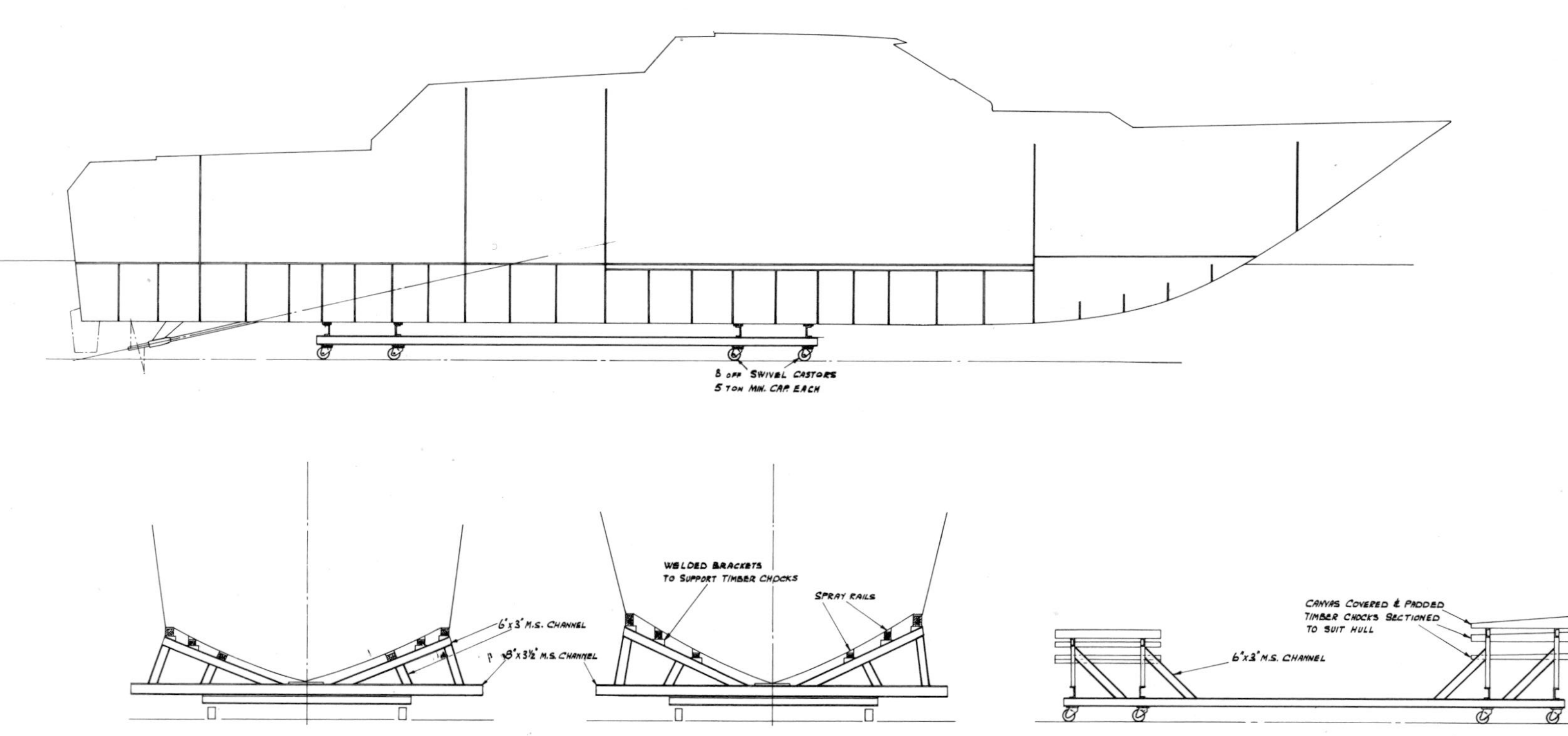

Q-2 *Launching trolley for 75 ft. boat.*

Slings

Depending on the weight of the vessel, the slings will be either fibre rope or flexible steel wire rope. Two slings are required, sufficiently long to go completely round the vessel, with enough extra length to reach a crane hook without too great an included angle between the forward and aft sling. Spreaders should be arranged just above the sheer between the sling legs, to prevent the slings from exerting a crushing load on the hull (see figure Q-3).

The crane hook will self-centre itself over the centre of gravity of the lifted weight. To ensure a level lift, the slings, if of equal length, should be positioned at equal distance forward and aft of the centre of gravity. Padding should be wrapped around the slings at points of contact with the hull to prevent damage and marking. Preventers should be secured to each sling leg around the end of the vessel, at about gunwale height, to prevent the sling from slipping inwards and so giving an unequal lift. Length of sling will also be dependent, of course, on possible maximum height of crane hook.

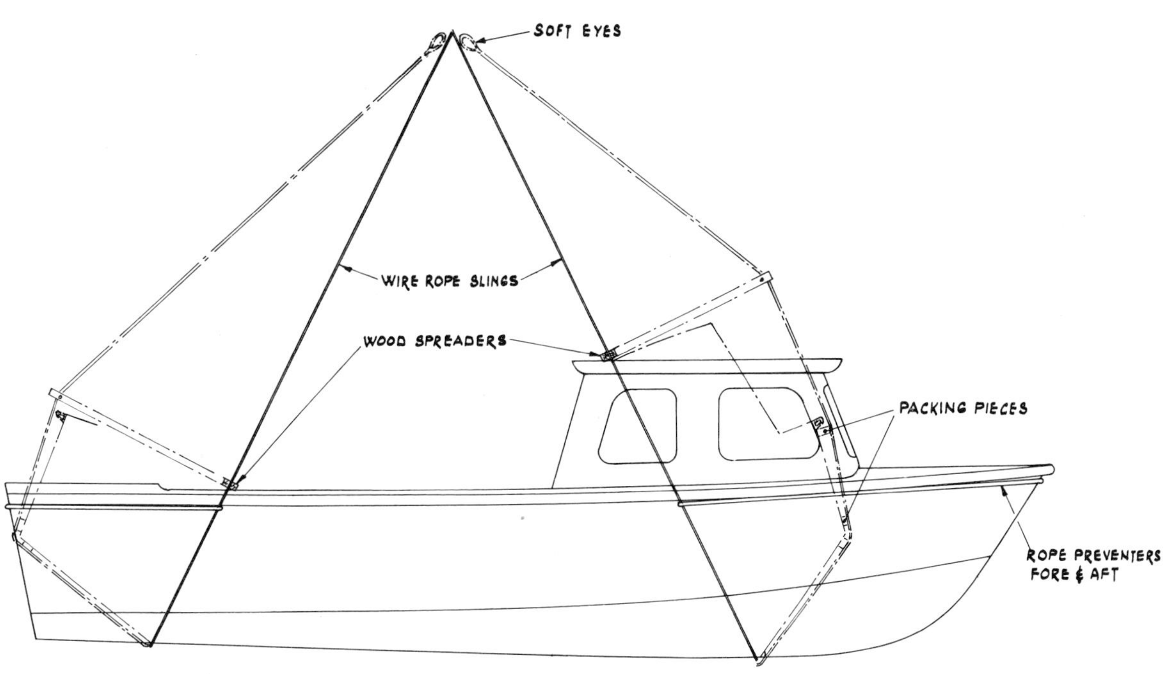

Q-3 *Around boat slings with spreaders.*

Gunwale plates

If it is likely that the vessel will be lifted in and out of the water frequently, the safest and most efficient method is to fit gunwale lifting plates. These normally consist of two or three legged steel plates bolted through the hull, either inside or outside, with the top of the plate extending just above the gunwale, to which the sling is attached by shackles. If possible, the plates should be positioned in way of bulkheads. If this is not possible, extra internal stiffening may be necessary to spread the stress imposed by lifting, to avoid a stress concentration in a weak area. It is possible, of course, by having slings of unequal length, to adjust for the crane hook to come above the boat centre of gravity and still maintain a level lift. To avoid unnecessary stress on the hull, spreaders between each sling should always be fitted, for both types of slinging. (see figure Q-4).

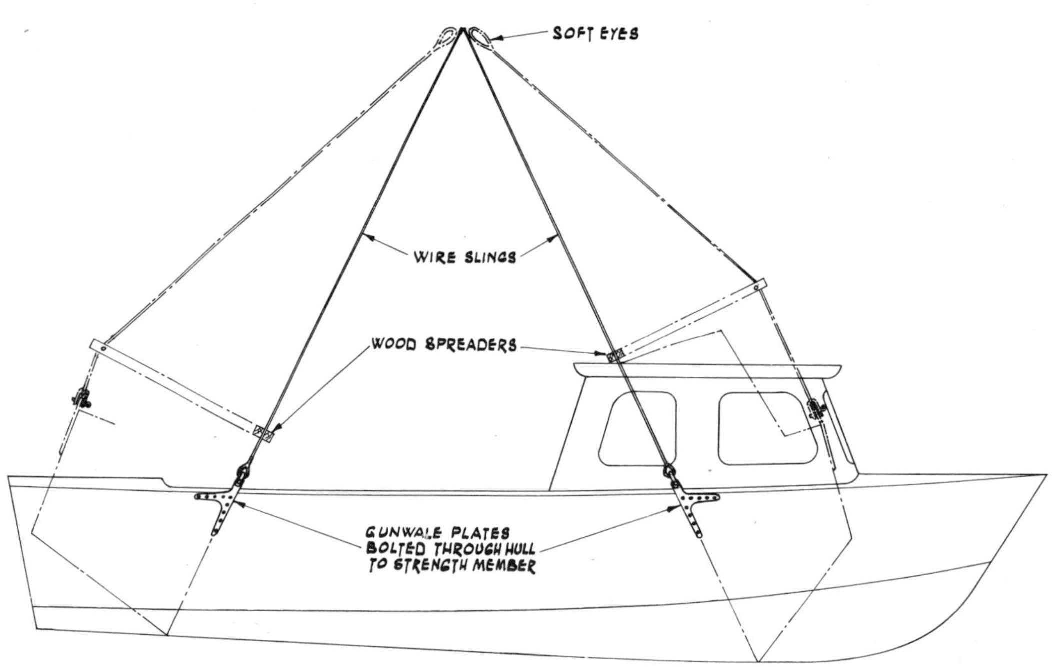

Q-4 *Gunwale slings.*

18 Hull Repairs

Marine-type aluminium alloys have a high degree of ductility; that is, they will deform or stretch as much as eight to fifteen percent before rupture. Because of this, the majority of hull repairs call for the dressing of dents, rather than repairing cracks or tears.

Small indentations can be faired by the judicious use of a rubber or hide headed mallet, with a wooden dolly held on the opposite side. The dent should be hammered around its periphery at first, then working in a circular direction, move toward the centre, where the deformation is greatest.

Care must be taken not to overwork the area, as the material will work harden to the extent that it will eventually crack. When the amount of deformation is too great to respond to the above treatment, it may help to heat the area with a soft flame played around the area. The combination of heating and hammering, provided neither are used excessively, will often have the desired effect.

Marine type alloys are little affected by local gentle heat, but unlike steel, do not change colour when heated. This makes it a little more difficult to control the heat, by not knowing the temperature of the affected zone. To give an indication of this, it is advisable to use temperature indicating crayons of about 400 and 500°F. Circles close to the centre of the deformation should be marked with the 500°F crayon and rings outside this central zone should be marked with the 400°F crayon. Heat should be applied until the crayon marks start to melt, then remove the heat and commence hammering. Further heating and hammering should be kept to a minimum.

When the fairing has been completed, the area should be cooled with a light douch of water. Where a very fair hull is required, as for instance on the bottom of racing hulls, slight depressions can be faired by the application of an epoxy resin such as Araldite. The metal must be degreased, abraded with emery cloth and then degreased again. Mixing and application should be to manufacturer's instructions.

Several thin coats should be applied in preference to a few thick coats. Curing can be accelerated by heating.

When fully cured, the surface sets rock hard and can be sanded to a very fine smooth finish.

Where the metal has actually torn, leaving a jagged edge, the metal should be dressed back as far as possible to the original shape. The area of the tear should be cut out including a generous margin all round, to ensure that any surface cracks that could propagate are removed, and a patch welded in position. When any doubt exists of the

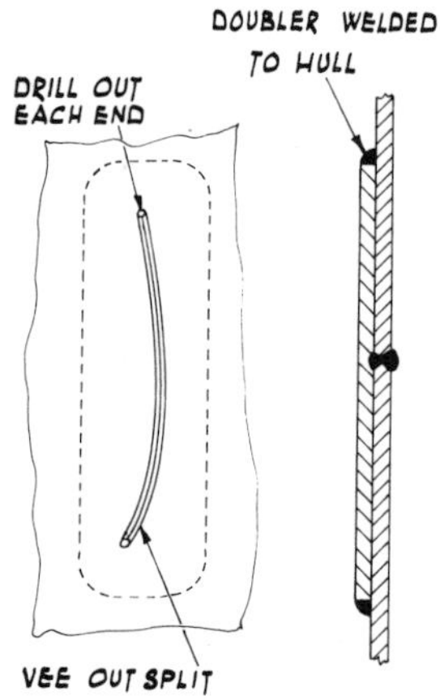

R-1 *Interior doubler welded to hull over split.*

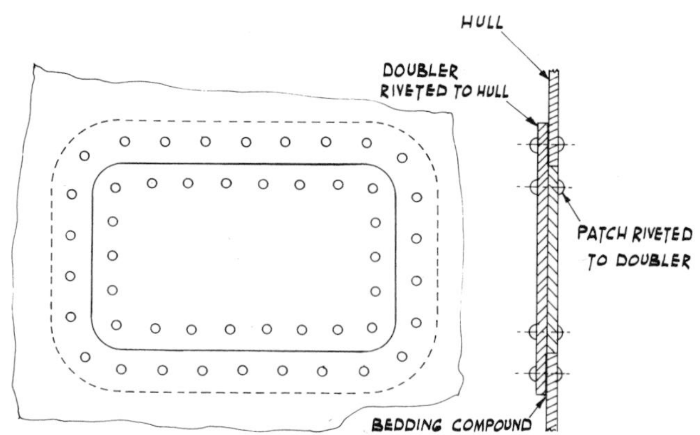

R-2 *Patch riveted when welding facility is not available.*

integrity of the metal local to the repair, an interior doubler can be welded in position, covering the doubtful area. (figure R-1). When the damaged plate is too thin for welding, or the welding facility is not available, the patch can be riveted in position. (figure R-2). For all underwater riveting, solid rivets or sealed type should be used, and all mating surfaces and rivet shanks should be coated with a suitable elastomer sealant. Where a very heavy blow has been sustained covering a large area, it is not often that an actual split in the metal will occur due to overstretching. Because of the extreme ductility there is more likely to be an excessive stretching of the metal and this tends to inhibit its return to the original shape, there being more area than originally. Where it is not desired to replace the damaged plate, it may be necessary to saw a slot in the centre of the dent. This provides room for metal displacement during the fairing process. The width of the slot will vary with the amount of stretching that has occurred.

One advantage with an aluminium hull is that, where a permanent set has occurred, the aluminium work-hardens because of the distortion, and its strength increases.

Further loading up to the amount that caused the original deformation will not result in further distortion because the metal is not weakened by the effect of stretching.

If the interior structure has suffered damage, this, if excessive, should be replaced rather than repaired. It is more difficult to 'lose' metal in extrusions than plate, and being usually harder material, will tend to resist re-forming.

19 Race Boats

Aluminium alloy is an ideal material for the larger classes of race boats. The precisely known mechanical characteristics enable the designer to produce a craft that will just withstand the stresses that are likely to be imposed upon it, without carrying the unnecessary weight penalties due to, say, a thicker layup than absolutely necessary to allow for possible laminator errors in glass reinforced plastic boats.

In race boats of all types, weight plays a most important part. The ratio of displacement to horsepower necessarily figures very largely in the designer's calculations.

S-1 *Gas turbine engined race boat travelling at about 80 m.p.h.*

At the present time, by far the majority of race boats of all classes are constructed in G.R.P. Increasingly, aluminium alloy is becoming popular with some of the top drivers in the 35 to 45 ft. offshore class. Surprisingly, nearly all of these boats are being built in England, and not as might be expected in the U.S.A. where the majority of the world's aluminium craft are presently constructed.

In racing, the object, depending on competition, must be to maintain maximum speed. In offshore racing, this sometimes includes maintaining high speeds in rough weather. It is during these times, that any weaknesses display themselves. It is not unknown for G.R.P. hull to commence de-lamination in severe weather, and on one occasion at least to lose an entire layer of skin. This sort of condition is impossible with an aluminium hull. It is also very unusual for the larger G.R.P. hulls to last for several seasons of hard racing as have several aluminium hulls.

With possible impact loads in excess of 20 G's in the bow areas, and with the ever increasing speeds and therefore even higher stress loadings, it seems reasonable that the designer must necessarily eventually insist upon a material that can provide him with precisely known mechanical characteristics. The ductility of the material is clearly shown in figure S-2.

S-2 Blitz *after crashing into the rocks at a reputed 70 m.p.h.*

The race boat *Blitz*, formerly *Miss Enfield 2*, whilst racing in the Cowes–Torquay–Cowes race of 1976, crashed into the rocks at a reputed 70 m.p.h. The starboard side which was riveted $\frac{1}{16}$ in. thick, and the bottom welded $\frac{3}{16}$ in. thick aluminium suffered distortion of about 3 in. deep at the centre. The bottom maintained its integrity with no fractures, the topsides pulled away slightly from the rivets. It is a fair assumption that, had the vessel been constructed of wood or G.R.P., the whole side and bottom would have been ripped out.

Evidence for the superiority of aluminium alloys where the strength weight ratio is of prime importance is found in the fact that aeroplanes, helicopters, hovercraft, hydrofoils—i.e., where aerodynamics play a significant role, are practically all built with a very high aluminium content.

Looking to the future, with the possible advent of Ground Effect Machines, and other structures where aerodynamic lift will be a major force in their efficiency, it seems inevitable that aluminium alloys will figure very largely, if not wholly, in the structure. Figure S-1 illustrates an aluminium hulled, gas turbine engined race boat travelling at about 80 m.p.h.

S-3 *Cutaway sketch of 50 knot tender.*

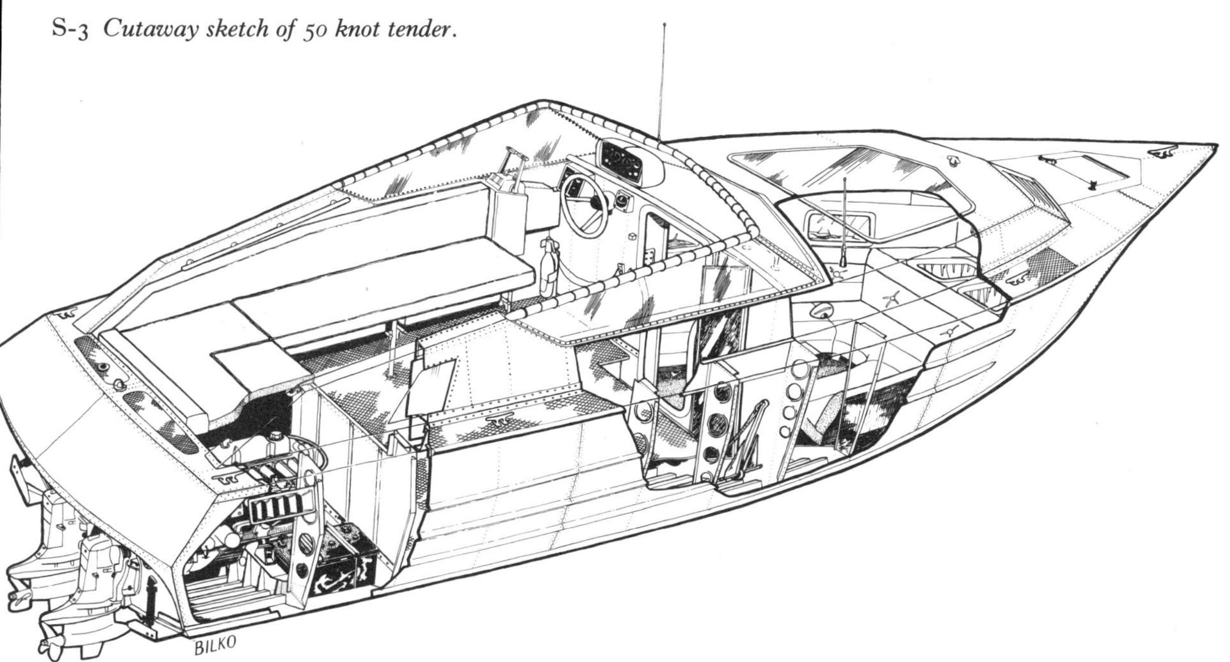

Index